IMPRISONED

FROM A VEIL OF SHAME TO A VEIL OF GLORY- ONE WOMAN'S JOURNEY

12/00
Love,
[signature]

By Patricia C. Harris

Psalms 3:3 — You are His Princess, Allow God to lift your head. Merry Christmas!

Spiritan Press
Carrollton, Texas

IMPRISONED

Copyright © 1999 by Patricia Cunningham Harris

Spiritan Press
P.O. Box 111103
Carrollton, TX 75011-1103

ISBN 0-9674868-0-7
Second Edition (Revised)

Cover Illustration by Sharon Neal

Printed by Mix Printing Company
2441 Midway Road
Carrollton, Texas 75006

To order copies:
Call: 972-939-0455
or write:
P.O. Box 111103
Carrollton, TX 75011-1103

Unless otherwise indicated, all Old and New Testament Scripture quotations are taken from The Amplified Bible, New International Version or The King James Version of the Holy Bible

Printed in the United States of America
All rights reserved under International Copyright Law.
Contents and/or cover may not be reproduced in whole or in part in any form without the express written consent of the publisher.

DEDICATION

Foremost, I dedicate this book to my precious Heavenly Father, my Lord and Savior, Jesus Christ, and the Holy Spirit who comforted me while I was "imprisoned."

Secondly, I wish to dedicate this book to my godly husband and the priest of our home, Eddie Harris, whose unconditional love served as the impetus I needed to begin my journey to wholeness. I love you with all my heart.

To my three children, Denyel, Earl and Amira, I say thank you for allowing me to write this book. Your father and I are especially grateful for your unified prayers that this written work will serve as an anointed conduit to heal hurting lives. I love you and thank you for your support.

To my parents, Bill and Mary Cunningham: Thank you for always being there. Both of you have stood beside me as I began my pilgrimage to wholeness. I want to thank you for believing in me enough to make an investment in this book. The first copies in print were a result of the seed you sowed. I love you both so much.

To my siblings, who kept loving me, kept believing in me and who never shunned me because of my failures, I say thank you, Sherrie, Rhonda and Billy.

To Pastors Mike and Kathy Hayes, thank you for the corporate mantle of grace, love and transparency through which you operate and which manifests and flows throughout our church body. Your ministry on the power of transparency has been rhema for me and consequently, life changing. I love you both.

To Bishop Nathaniel and Pastor Valerie Holcomb: Christian House of Prayer became a refuge center for me, a shelter from the storm. Your ministry and your unconditional love initiated the foundation for my return to the Kingdom of God. I love you two from my heart.

Finally, I dedicate this autobiography to each woman whose life parallels my own painful indiscretions and moral failings. I pray that you experience wholeness, transformed in the likeness of Father God who created you with purpose and dignity. In the presence of God and by the authority of Jesus Christ, I declare that you shall be set free! The chains are broken! You, too, are free to be "the unashamed woman" through the atoning blood of Jesus!

Dance before His presence with great joy, bow at His feet and adore Him, for He adores you and He loves you with an "everlasting love". You are His Princess, His Jewel, and the Sparkle in His eye.

Patricia C. Harris

ACKNOWLEDGEMENTS

Thank you to the following women who submitted a prayer for inclusion in this book: Evangelist Mary Cunningham, Pastor Melinda Manning, Pastor Amy Hossler, Pastor Derozette Banks and Pastor Jessye Ruffin. Please know that your prayers will impact countless lives for eternity.

A special thank you to my editor and sister, Sherrie Copeland. Your editorial skill and style have enhanced the quality of this book. Thank you for juggling your schedule and meeting the deadlines. You have always stood beside me and supported me. Thank you for being there once again. And to your husband, Jim, thank you for sharing Sherrie during the times I needed her most. I love you both.

Thank you, Pastor Jessye Ruffin, you have been there to walk with me through the emotional turbulence I experienced as a result of soul-ties and the presence of darkness in my life. Thank you for your counseling and your guidance. Pastor Jerry Ruffin, I want to thank you for your spiritual insight and your warfare. You both have been my mentors and my friends. I love you.

As my elders, Wayne and Jill Blue, you have covered me in prayer and stood by me as I shared the progressive stages of this book. Thanks for being there for me and for Eddie when we needed your support and counseling. I love you both.

Zone 1 Leaders, thank you for setting the atmosphere which released me to share my story in your presence. I love each of you.

To my illustrator, Sharon Neal, thank you for captivating my expressed thoughts and artistically portraying an illustrative piece which not only conveys my 12 year imprisonment, but my subsequent victory as well!

To Billy, as a screenwriter, your knowledge and insight have been invaluable. Thank you for your advice and for taking the time to review my work. I love you.

To Ira, thank you for your comments and review. Rhonda, thank you for always believing in me. I love you both.

Pastor Jerry Parsons, thank you for your encouragement and advice as I began the process for putting my story into literary form.

To Ginny Autry and Jackie Powell, thank you for standing with me in the Spirit and for encouraging me to move forward with the completion of this book.

A special thank you to David James. Your expertise and knowledge were invaluable to me. Thank you, Christy, for supporting David as he invested his time and skills in this work.

A special thank you to Darryl Mix and Mix Printing, Inc. Thank you for granting me a favor and for believing in me. Darryl, I want to especially thank you for your time, your expertise, and for hearing the Heart of God. God bless you.

Pastor Amy, my teacher, mentor and friend: Thank you for adhering to the voice of God as you obediently ministered to the "Band Of Women." Your impartation of God's Word has changed my life for eternity. I love you.

Contents

Dedication iii
Acknowledgements v
Foreword x
Preface xii
Introduction xiv

Section One
The Fall of Man (Woman) (Number Two in Scripture) 1

Chapter 1
    The Divorce 3
Chapter 2
    The Seed 7
Chapter 3
    The Affair 11
Chapter 4
    The Meeting 19

Section Two
God's Grace
(Number Five in Scripture) 27

Chapter 5
The Quandary 29

Chapter 6
The Prodigal Daughter 35

Chapter 7
He Gave Me A New Name 39

Chapter 8
My Knight In Shining Armor 45

Chapter 9
God's Amazing Grace 53

Chapter 10
The Past Returns 59

Chapter 11
The Unexpected 63

Chapter 12
The Presence Of Evil 69

Chapter 13
The Letter 77

Chapter 14
Tension In The Camp 79

Chapter 15
My Alabaster Box 83

Section Three
Finality/Conclusion
(Number Nine in Scripture) 87

Chapter 16
Saturated With His Word 89

Chapter 17
The Audible Voice Of God 95

Chapter 18
The Powerless Veil Of Shame 99

Chapter 19
Unashamed 101

Chapter 20
Hurting Women, Healed Lives 107

Chapter 21
Conclusion 111

Epilogue 115

Prayers Of Agreement 117
   A Prayer Reflecting God's Faithfulness 118
   Prayer Of Repentance For The Single 119
   A Prayer For Self-Forgiveness 120
   Prayer Of Displacement For Youth/Teens 122
   A Prayer For Destroying Soul-Ties 124

FOREWORD

Dear Readers,

The Lord's desire is for every believer to possess his own soul with His steadfastness of heart (Luke 21:19). I have known Patricia Harris (Trisha) for ten years as her spiritual counselor. I have stood by her as she recovered her soul from the contamination of the enemy. I have observed her forge herself through all of Satan's schemes against her and be victorious. There were times when she felt like she couldn't take any more attacks but as she has now learned, it took all of her trials and tribulations to build the honorable character and deep fortitude of soul that she possesses. If she were to take away even a microscopic portion of her life, she would not be the tremendous spiritual warrior for the Gospel that she is. It took all of her past emotional pain and heartache in order for the Holy Spirit to fashion her into the shining light that she has become.

Many of us have a shameful past that we are not proud of but few of us have the courage and strength to sacrificially help others by writing it in a book. "Trisha" is a very courageous woman of God who felt that if Jesus could die on the cross for mankind's reconciliation to the Father, then she could bear the cross of writing this book about not only her failures with the enemy, but also her great victories over the enemy.

I believe that many women will be set free from demons that have been assigned to viciously attack their sexuality which is the essence of how we reflect God, since man was created in His image. Satan's desire was to strip "Trisha" of all her self-esteem and God-esteem in the area of how she perceived herself as a woman of God. The enemy attacks women daily and lies to them about what they think about themselves, what others think of them and how the Lord perceives them. If the enemy can strip us of our sexuality then he has stripped us of the God within us and perverted our purpose.

Satan was unsuccessful in his war against "Trisha" and Eddie and he will be unsuccessful in his attack against you. "Trisha's" story will provoke you to repent and turn away from the supposedly safety in sensual living on those dead-end streets of life. These avenues in life have been diabolically created by familiar spirits whose only goal is to destroy you. If Satan needs to use a man of God to carry out his schemes against you, he will. We need all that Jesus has for us. Jesus came to set all of us free from the bondage of sin and He is the only way to recovery.

Jessye Ruffin, Associate Pastor
Covenant Church, Dallas, TX

PREFACE

As I first began to write this book, I struggled with the fact that its contents would expose in startling detail the shameful acts I performed against God, against the body of Christ and against my family, all of whom I love very much.

Inwardly, I remained unresolved regarding my decision to disclose my wretched "12 year secret". During this time of indecision my thoughts drifted back to how, in the midst of my turmoil, I often yearned to read a book written by a godly woman who had traveled the same agonizing path that I had experienced firsthand. I longed to scan the shelves of a Christian bookstore and find available resources and reading material by another woman like myself—a woman who actually overcame the shame, disgrace and condemnation of sexual impurity.

Dear Reader, the impurity to which I refer was an impurity that I willfully chose *after* I became a Christian. No, no one snatched my purity from me. Nor can I honestly attribute prior family background, or even ignorance as justification for my subsequent descent into the debauchery and forbidden lust of the flesh that I permitted into my life. Rather, as a woman of God, born again and spirit-filled, I chose to forsake my purity and my relationship with God for an adulterous relationship with a married man—<u>a married man who was, in fact, my pastor.</u>

I have repeatedly struggled with the disclosure of my painful past while writing these solemn words. Yet, I have also simultaneously sensed in my spirit, victory— victory that I now boldly proclaim looms upon the horizon for countless women seeking shelter from the same storms that assailed my own life.

For those of you who read the words of this book and who can relate personally or indirectly, yes, undoubtedly, we did defile ourselves. We have, in fact, experienced moral and spiritual failure in our lives, and as a result, we hurt our loved ones, ourselves, and our heavenly Father. And, yes, many of us have lived with insufferable guilt, deep-seated pain and self-condemnation because of it. But, I declare to you this moment, in spite of all this, because of Christ's shed blood on Calvary, you can be adorned in a veil of glory <u>if you are willing</u> to release all of your past to Him.

So, regardless of the option available to me to maintain anonymity and forego the writing of the following pages, I have chosen instead, to boldly pen the subsequent chapters in obedience to God's voice. He has inspired me to write my story as a testimony so others might overcome. In actuality, <u>"IMPRISONED"</u> is from Him, to every hurting woman who has ever experienced the shame of sexual impurity at any level. To those who are or have been entangled in a stronghold of lust or infidelity or who may even be on the verge of making such a decision, God has ordained that this book be written for you. No longer do you have to bear the weight of your shame.

You can truly be free through Jesus!

INTRODUCTION

This book represents the true, startling, revelatory account of how I, wounded, betrayed, scarred with genital herpes and a single parent of two little children, ages three and four, walked away from a ten year physically and emotionally abusive marriage. From there, poor decisions, immense vulnerability and my innate <u>willingness</u> to believe the devil's lies sent me headlong into a sexual relationship with my pastor—scarring me in such a way that it would hinder God's anointing in my life. Consequently, I would carry the weight of that guilt for twelve long years. Feeling inadequate, slimy and worthless, I invisibly wallowed under the overwhelming, ominous clouds of heaviness, self-reproach, guilt, shame and condemnation. When I ultimately found the strength to sever the relationship with my pastor, I had nowhere to go, no one to turn to. My immediate family (parents and siblings), always so supportive, were a thousand miles away—in other states. I felt so alone....

I believe that the denigrating shame associated with sexual impurity is one that women find hard to face because it demeans "the lady" in them. Ladies are viewed as pure, graceful, gentle, kind, wholesome, sound, polite, gracious, adorable, neat, well adorned ... and the list goes on. So how can a woman who has committed an act of sexual impurity, especially with a married man, ever feel like she deserves the right to be called a "lady"? Even worse, what happens when that act occurs with a married man who is also ... her pastor?

Somehow I told myself that I could get over it—that it was behind me now, that it wasn't all my fault. Yet, for years I carried the burden and the shame inside a broken vessel. Nevertheless, God kept on loving me and never gave up on my future.

By not knowing who I was in Christ, I felt as though I was just a number, a person without a name, a prisoner. One of Satan's greatest plans is to deceive us by clouding our view of who God says we are in His Word. Being greatly deceived, I bought the devil's lies that I was just a number, an insignificant being. However, I later learned that being "just a number" could be a powerful statement from God's perspective. The biblical connotation of numbers are symbolic in the heart of God. **2-5-9** are relevant to my 12-year journey. While **two** refers to the "fall of man", **five** is the number of "grace or favor for the unworthy" and **nine** symbolizes the "conclusion of a matter." In essence, this numerical combination summarizes the events that took place in my life - a _fallen_ woman who experiences the _grace_ of God and the victorious _conclusion_ to a 12-year, private imprisonment. Thus, the numbers **2-5-9** can be significant to all of us. Although you may have _fallen_, there is yet God's bountiful _grace_ by which your _conclusion_ can be victorious through Christ Jesus.

So when satan tries to tell you that you are "just a number", just tell him you know where you've been and you know where you're going, and unlike him, your _conclusion_ ends in victory through the redemptive blood of Jesus! (Reference Resource: E.W.Bullinger. _Number In Scripture._ Grand Rapids, MI.: Kregel Publications, 1967)

Today, I am a victorious overcomer and God wants the same for you! I would like to share with you the journey I traveled from my veil of shame to my veil of glory. As you read my story you will see how the hand of God guided me. God cares just as much for your victory as He does for mine. My triumphs can be your triumphs, too. I ask that you envision yourself coming out of your situation with a shout of victory. God is an awesome God. He reigns from Heaven above with wisdom, power and love. He is such an awesome God. He cares for you and me.

Section One
The Fall of Man (Woman) (Number Two in Scripture)

CHAPTER 1
THE DIVORCE

Like many young girls, I, too, dreamed of growing up, getting married to a tall, dark handsome "Knight in Shining Armor," raising children and living happily ever after. During my adolescence, my thoughts often drifted to such a make-believe, fantasy world. In my spare moments, I would write countless short stories, in which my main characters, usually a young, beautiful girl and a knight in shining armor, would marry at the plot's conclusion and live long, fulfilling prosperous lives.

I believe that I had finally fulfilled my dreams when I married my high school sweetheart at the tender age of nineteen. My marriage, however, failed to be the fantasy I envisioned as a child. I found myself married to a very wounded man. A man who was hurting from unmet needs in his childhood. There were so many unresolved issues....the premature death of his mother while he was yet a little boy, a grieving alcoholic father who abdicated his parental responsibilities, and additionally, the loss of what once was a family knitted together....later tragically divided throughout his childhood and adolescent years.

After nine years of an abusive marital relationship to this man, I became a divorcee with two small children, financial indebtedness and immense, insufferable, emotional baggage. With only a year of college and limited skills, I joined one of the fastest growing groups in the country ... single parents.

Prior to our divorce, my husband, whom I will call Fred Weaver, and I had sought marital counseling from our pastor. This same pastor, incidentally, had also provided pastoral leadership to my husband and I when we lived in another state.

Amid several years of job relocations and transfers, our paths crossed and, once again, we found ourselves attending his church. As a result of those years of mutual acquaintance, we had fostered a friendship with this pastor and his wife.

Though Fred and I had previously pursued secular counseling in the past, no tangible results or noticeable change had occurred in our marriage. No matter which counselor I selected, Fred expressed open disdain, disinterest and an unwillingness to be transparent. In fact, he even indicated his disinterest in seeking marital guidance from our pastor. However, in this instance, I unflinchingly insisted that both he and I pursue pastoral counseling if we were to save our "dangling by a thread" marriage.

So, with Fred reluctantly in tow, we attended several counseling sessions with the Pastor and his wife. Even when his wife was unable to attend, the Pastor would still meet with the two of us. It appeared, however, to be a losing battle. Eventually, I reported Fred to the authorities for his continued physical violence. He was later removed from our home and I found myself alone with our two small children.

My family, made aware of the marital separation, tried to offer as much support as possible. My mother, a devoted believer and praying woman, would call, pray for me and counsel me long distance. My parents, as well as my siblings, sent monies to help assist me in my financial struggles. They helped as much as they could, but they all lived far away. Now, alone and a thousand miles from home, I faced the feelings of rejection, abandonment and the debilitating aftermath of an emotionally draining and physically abusive marriage.

Additionally, the infidelity introduced in our marriage by Fred and then later, by me, had left me with a severe case of genital herpes. Before our marriage dissolved, I discovered that Fred was a carrier and that I had contracted the dreadful disease from him. In all honesty, I could not place all of the blame on him, as we were both guilty of extra-marital affairs and as a result, we were reaping what we had sown. So, here I was, not only a single parent of a four year old daughter and three year old son, but also a battered casualty of an abusive marriage, left wounded, betrayed and scarred with genital herpes. Unfortunately, from this point on, I would continue to make poor decisions, the consequences of which I would bear for years to come.

THE DIVORCE

Where do I go? Is there anywhere to hide?
I feel lonely, afraid, so barren inside.
I have two little children without their dad
My situation—so frightening, so hopeless, so sad

Alone, yet not alone, for God can lead the way
He alone can guide me with each decision made
Suddenly I decided to handle it on my own
So I turned away from God and no longer sought His throne

The spirit of darkness entered - it felt like a horrible curse
Keeping God out of the equation only made matters worse
It would be 12 years later that I would lift my eyes,
forgive myself and finally arise...
to walk in victory

CHAPTER 2
THE SEED

After my husband's removal from our home, the pastor who had provided ongoing counseling to us during our marital difficulties, stopped by to check on my kids and me. Though not yet divorced, Fred had filed the papers to initiate the process, and I was in total agreement with his decision. I no longer desired to keep our destructive relationship together. It had become an effort in futility.

On one occasion when the Pastor, whom I will simply refer to as "Pastor", called me on the phone, he mentioned to me that his wife had accused him of being interested in me because of his continued involvement in my life. I, at that point, had never even considered the thought. When I addressed him as Pastor, I thought of him only in that regard. I was to soon discover, however, that the Pastor had, in fact, thought of me beyond what was considered appropriate. When he stated to me what his wife was thinking, I felt a sense of embarrassment and told him "oh no, that would be horrible". I suggested to the Pastor that I talk with his wife to reassure her. (At that time, my youth, naivete and immaturity clouded my perceptions of the Pastor's apparent intentions toward me).

Though Pastor's wife was a radiant woman, I later found out that she was also very wounded and broken, and with good reason. She distrusted her husband and intentionally distanced herself from many women, to include me. Though I had known her for years and was fond of her, she did not pursue a close relationship with me. Later, I would discover why.

Pastor, on the other hand, was quite the opposite. He was everyone's friend. He knew everyone and everyone knew him. He was well liked by both men and women and garnered respect in the community. Overall, Pastor possessed an enviable reputation (I have since discovered the difference between *reputation* and *character*. *Reputation* is who people think you are, while *character* is who you are when no one is looking).

In addition to his pastoral calling, Pastor previously held such prestigious positions as Bishop (where he assumed oversight over numerous churches). He also served as a board member of several reputable community organizations. Coupled with these outward accolades, Pastor possessed dynamic wit, charm and charisma. He could mingle with any group and present his ideas and opinions with authority. As a result, he often successfully manipulated or exerted control in many situations. In the midst of her husband's unabashed popularity and favor, Pastor's wife would often stand by silently on the sidelines. She had evolved into a very insecure woman because, as I later discovered, Pastor's underlying ultimatum to her, regarding his lifestyle, was "either take it or leave it". Obviously, she decided to "take it".

After Pastor had disclosed his wife's feelings and I responded with denial that such a thing could occur, he inquired as to why I would think such a situation would be repugnant. He queried me with such questions as "Do you think I am too old? "Would it be that bad?" "What's wrong with me?" "Am I ugly?" And, with a chuckle, he would unabashedly add, "I know I am good lookin'."

I flushed, embarrassed by his direct questioning. Despite his candid questioning and comments, which caught me off guard, I was flattered that this man would consider me; not just a mere man-but **the Pastor**. (In retrospect, I now realize this was due to my own intense inferiority complex coupled with my unresolved, deep-seated emotional baggage and failure to realize who I was in Christ) The seed of lust was planted in his heart and a seed of illicit excitement took form in mine that would eventually lead to my spiraling descent into the throes of an illicit affair and 12 years of self-condemnation.

SOMEBODY WANTS ME

*What could this new found feeling be that
Has awakened within me
A feeling of hope, a feeling of intrigue,
A feeling of somebody wants me,*

*Somebody really wants me.
The grass looks greener now than it ever has,
The birds sing a new song, the sky radiates a pure blue
And somebody really wants me.
It's big him and little me. He's willing to risk it all, for me?*

*What is it that makes him look at me?
Who am I that he would consider me?
He really wants me, I can feel it.
I must adorn myself, I can live again.
For someone knocks at my door.
Someone sweetly, enticingly calls out my name
Dead emotions, alive again, because somebody wants me.*

*It feels good, but it doesn't.
It seems right, but it isn't.
I feel bold, yet I feel ashamed.
I want in,
But I want out.*

*I know what I want,
but I am so confused.
I want to pray, but I can't.
I want to win, but I am losing ... and, inwardly, I know it.*

*God is there and so is Satan.
God is reaching, Satan is pulling.
God says "come"... Satan says "don't listen"
God says "come"... Satan says "Someone is waiting for you"
God says "come"... Satan says "Somebody finally wants you".*

*And I say "... but he wants me, he really wants me..."
I'm left to face despondency, to face despair, yet all I can
consider is that "somebody really wants me."*

CHAPTER 3
THE AFFAIR

After a few more visits from the Pastor, the affair began. The Pastor knew that I had genital herpes because I had disclosed this very intimate detail to him during the prior marital counseling sessions. But he told me that he did not care. I was puzzled at his response concerning this incurable disease and the potential risk of transference.

The physical side of our illicit relationship began at his request and continued at his request. The affection we shared was purely lust and based on deception. But as a "needy" person at this point in my life, it met the yearning to feel significant and of value. The deception I was under provoked me to believe I was special to the pastor and that he really needed me. However, as I later discovered, he was driven by his physical and emotional desires and I merely served as a conduit. In other words, I was not special to him, just available.

Often, I thought to myself ... "What are you doing and why? He is a married man, not your high school sweetheart!!! Worst yet, <u>he is</u> your Pastor." The slime and the guilt began to pile upon me like a weight. A cloud of heaviness moved in and I felt myself literally connect with an unclean spirit. My body, once the temple of the Holy Spirit (1 Cor. 6:18), now represented utter defilement and uncleanness. I wanted out, yet I wanted to stay in. "This man needs me and I want to be there for him" became my way of thinking.

Each time we had physical contact, the darkness in my soul grew darker and the gaping hole of emptiness I felt inside increased. What I had been seeking all my life seemed to continue to elude me, to be so out of reach. I sought a romantic relationship with someone who would listen to my dreams and my goals. I yearned for someone to love and cherish me. In retrospect, I realize now that Pastor was also obviously experiencing a lot of pain and I was simply his first aid kit. I was a pseudo pain reliever for him. He searched for, reached out and demanded more than I could ever possibly give.

So here we were, two needy people—a pastor and one of his sheep. Both of us, in dire need of a Savior, sought refuge from the storm, but in the wrong place, in the wrong way and void of God's divine plan. How often we all turn to pseudo pain relievers for a quick fix, when all we have to do is turn to Jesus. No matter the problem, for each of us, the right answer awaits us through Jesus Christ. For, His blood paid the ultimate price.

As I earlier stated, the Pastor and I had our first physical encounter after he had visited me on several occasions. After the initial illicit liaison occurred, he asked me to drop the title of "Pastor" and call him by his first name. He joked about the fact that we were sleeping together and I was yet calling him "Pastor". The ease with which this Pastor approached our relationship was beyond me. Unfortunately, over the years his heart had grown very cold and there appeared to be no inner conviction on his part regarding his behavior. Seemingly unaffected, he appeared totally oblivious to the fact that we were actually having an "affair" and acted as though all was "normal".

I experienced inexplicable depravity and accompanying feelings of nausea after that first physical encounter with the Pastor. After he left my apartment, I sat down to contemplate the gravity of my choice and my actions. What had I done? I felt bad, but I also felt as though he might really love me (how blind I was, for this was yet another deceptive thought planted by the enemy). In the spirit realm, I began a rapid descent into a bottomless demonic abyss. Even when I wanted to do what was right and good, evil

The Affair

was ever present with me and I became subject to its insistent demands (Romans 7:21). I blindly interpreted Pastor's advances as "he needs me."

In prior counseling sessions Pastor had told Fred and me that, to add excitement to his sex life, he would watch sex channels on cable network because it made him do "crazy things" and heightened his sex drive. He insinuated that to view such channels (in the sanctity of one's bedroom) would add spice to our relationship. (Pastor never appeared to feel any conviction about viewing pornography, nor did it seem he perceived it as sinful activity. However, unrealized strongholds were being established in the spirit realm, and he was indeed a victim). During our first year of marriage, Fred and I engaged in viewing pornography on videos, in magazines and in literature. We, too, had become victims to its alluring, enticing grip. However, after I began attending church regularly, I felt convicted about viewing it and over time, I stopped. Yet, this Pastor endorsed it as being okay for married couples. "The bed is undefiled when you are married" was his justification. Since it was already a stronghold in our lives, Pastor's endorsement encouraged us to keep this particular "sin pattern" active in our marriage. At that time in my immature walk with God, I did not have the revelation that pornography was a stronghold. I had not been involved in a church that imparted such teaching. In fact, I had never heard anyone minister or preach on the specific types of "strongholds". However, inwardly I felt it was wrong and would come under conviction when viewing it.

In later years, I learned through the teaching of God's Word that those who walk according to the flesh will fulfill the lust of the flesh and will forsake "all" for just one opportunity of fleeting pleasure. It was this same spirit of lust, this very same stronghold that guided the Pastor and me to forsake "our relationship with God" to pursue quick, forbidden encounters.

In addition, Pastor disclosed to me that he suffered from haunting childhood issues. He was born illegitimately as a product of an unfortunate, perverted relationship. Furthermore, a background of homosexuality, infidelity and pornography (as stated earlier) only exacerbated the emotional baggage silently carried by Pastor. Despite these grievous problems, this wounded man acknowledged the call on his life to be God's oracle. However, the enemy had deceptively stepped in to rob him of this call.

I did not understand "soul ties" ... but, later, as I progressed in a true Christian walk, I discovered that all the people Pastor had ever slept with were now tied to my soul – and mine to his...a transference of souls. I was getting deeper and deeper into a tangled web of spirits from which only God could deliver me. However, at the time, I did not realize this was happening. I just wanted to be a comforter for Pastor. He needed me and I needed him...and so I used this rationale to justify my sinful actions.

Pastor began calling me at night so he could arrange to stop by or either request I meet him at a specific place. He insisted I find a babysitter so that he could see me often. It appeared that he was increasingly becoming emotionally and physically attached to me. He wanted to be around me all the time. Conversely, his emotional attachment fed a need in me to be wanted as a woman. He called me several times a day to see how I was doing. He purchased gifts for me—expensive gifts that I could never afford. The incessant latching of demonic spirits upon my soul deepened and I began to sell out ...but not completely ... because I never had any peace. Constantly, I would wrestle with guilt and shame. I could never really justify my actions or motives, because I knew I was wrong.

On the other hand, I could never understand the carefree attitude of Pastor. He was always happy to see me. He would whistle, sing, and share details about upcoming church services and his plans for church growth. It was as if we were walking in unity as husband and wife. My soul yearned to be needed, to be important, to be included. The Pastor met that need as he sought my advice and discussed with me the details of "church business". I could never quite grasp or understand his casual approach to our affair. (Maybe it was because I was not his first mistress, and none of this was new to him). I had never been involved with a married man and worst yet a pastor; therefore I was not prepared for the constant deceit, scheming and lying that had to be incorporated into my day to day activities in order for meetings and schedules to be planned, arranged and rearranged. There is no way I could describe the knot that stayed in my stomach because of my newly acquired lifestyle. Yet, it was all I had, and so I just kept holding on. We would sometimes meet at hotels during the day. We would actually go to hotels in the city in which we both resided. I was always a nervous wreck regarding the deception and the sneaking around. Yet, Pastor made light of it and appeared to see each rendezvous as another opportunity to sit on his throne. (The enemy wants sin to be exciting, risky, fun, daring ... and then he crashes in on your parade and laughs at your flagrant stupidity). The Pastor's philosophy for avoiding rumors was to meet at a local spot. He stated rumors are started when you "appear" to be sneaking around. He believed if you were bold about it, people wouldn't question it. Therefore, he believed that to be as conspicuous as possible would distract attention. Baffled, I would then ask him, "if they see us coming out of a hotel together, or even see our cars parked at a hotel, won't that be a clue?" He answered assuredly, "Unless they catch us in the act, they can't prove anything." I remained in awe of Pastor's ability to staunchly uphold his point of view and remain in control of any situation.

Throughout our affair, I continued to attend Pastor's church where I would listen to him preach God's Word. I asked him on several occasions, "How can you preach God's Word and yet have an affair with me? Aren't you afraid? Don't you feel guilty?" He would patiently respond by telling me that God knew he was a man and that men have needs. He told me God also knew how unhappy he was with his wife and that God wanted him to be happy. He explained to me that God doesn't sit up in the sky with a big hammer ready to bang us on the head just because we sin. Rather, he assured me that God loved both of us and He understood our need to be loved.

After hearing his justification regarding our sinful actions, I clearly remember thinking, that this answer was worse than the reply he gave for being conspicuous when we went to local hotels.

Sometimes at home, I would just sit in silence and contemplate what I was doing, and in disbelief, I would just shake my head. Darkness was closing in on me and I knew it.

I GAVE IT ALL AWAY

All I had to do was trust Him.
He asked so little of me and from me.
When I cried He wanted to hold me
Yet, to a pastor's arms I went instead

God had the answers
Yet, I sought my own simple solutions
He saw my mistakes
and still He wanted to hold me

At one time I knew my Lord face to face.
I was getting closer to Him
But then I pulled away
And, instead, followed the voice of the deceiver

I gave it all away,
I forsook all for nothing in return
God saw my sins, my broken heart
Yet, He still wanted to hold me.

When I wept, He wept with me.
He reached for me, and I turned away
"Just look at me now", I said, my head cast down
I have nothing to offer, nothing to give

Yet, He still reached out
To hold me close.
Jesus wanted to hold me. I drew back—
Not now, I can't...just look at me!

He looked at me, and I felt his gaze follow me.
Go away please... "I'm not worthy"... I turned to leave—
Yet, when I looked back
He was still reaching for me.

CHAPTER 4
THE MEETING

One evening after an "encounter" with Pastor, and approximately 45 minutes after he left my house, the phone rang. I heard his voice when I picked up the receiver. He told me that he was home in bed but that his wife was not there. He expressed suspicion that she might be looking for him and heaved a sigh of relief that he left my home when he did. Just as I mentioned my hope that she not come over to my house, I suddenly heard a knock at my door.

I spoke into the receiver to Pastor, "Someone is at my door." Pastor instructed me, "Answer the door, I will stay on the line." I laid the phone down on my bed and went to answer the knock. It was Pastor's wife. I numbly opened the door. Pastor's wife asked if her husband was there.

I told her "No". She asked to come in. I let her in. She looked around and then looked at me. She asked if Pastor had been in my home. I lied, "No". Awkwardly, I offered her a seat. She then sat down at my kitchen table and I sat across from her. She looked me in the eyes and asked me point blank... "Are you having an affair with my husband?" "No," I again lied. She then confessed to me that she felt Pastor was interested in me.

As she continued to talk to me, I found myself staring into the hurt and sad eyes that pierced mine from across my table that night. I will never forget looking at the wife of this pastor, nor will I ever forget her almost grievous accusation in the form of an inquiry: "Are you having an affair with my husband?" That question silently stabbed my heart. It was the most degrading, humiliating thing I had ever been asked ... yet I deserved every question she hurled at me, for I alone had disgraced and debased myself by my lurid lifestyle and wrong choices. Her heart was broken and her sorrow grievous. I was to blame. I was the "other woman."

All of a sudden it became all too clear why she was withdrawn, why she avoided women ... who could she trust? I had known her for several years, and now I, too, had "stabbed" her. Once again, this pastor's wife was experiencing betrayal. A feeling that I believe she knew, all too well.

I will never forget her sad eyes as she looked straight into mine during our conversation. Oh, how I wanted to turn away or hold my head down in shame, but I did not. Instead, I looked straight at her as I silently fought back the tears. The pain in her was so obvious. Most distressing of all was that I knew I was responsible for her breaking heart.

But she never cried, she just painfully returned my gaze. She remained calm, though I knew she was crushed, her burden seemingly too immense, too heavy to carry any further.

As I looked at her, I wondered how many times she had traveled this road. I thought of how she had to humble herself to knock on my door to ask if her own husband was at another woman's house. She got up after saying a few more words and started toward the door. She turned to me and said, "If he comes over here, tell him I am looking for him". I nodded my head. Then she left. I knew that she knew.

After I closed the door behind her stooped, departing frame, I went back to my bedroom where I picked up the phone. Almost numb from the experience, I whispered, still in a daze, "It was your wife, she just left."

Pastor then wanted to know what was said. I told him we would talk about it later and that I had to go. I then hung up the phone.

There are no words that I can use to describe the sickening dismay and inner pain and grief I experienced from that meeting with the Pastor's wife. What had I become? I thought. How could I sleep with Pastor, attend his church, and then sit across from his wife and boldly lie. God have mercy on my wretched soul! Who was I? I used to be a Christian woman who had earned the respect of others, I knew God and the power of His resurrection, I used to experience His presence ... but now His presence could not be felt, it could not be found, I felt so all alone. All I could do was just put my face in my hands. I felt sick, sick, sick, sick. I wanted that pastor's wife to reach out to me, to hold me as I begged her forgiveness. I wanted to cry and tell her "I am so sorry". I wanted to confess to her what I had done. I was sooooo ashamed. She had been in search of her husband ... the pastor ... at my house! God help me, I thought.

That night, something began to change in me. I knew that somehow I had to get out of this relationship in spite of what Pastor said or felt. As I sat there thinking of how to tell him, my mind traveled back to our numerous talks. I had previously mentioned to Pastor that we had to end our affair. But Pastor declared emphatically that he wouldn't be able to make it if I left him. He was so convincing, and he always made me feel guilty as though I was betraying him by even making the suggestion. As I sat there all alone in my living room that night, I groped for answers. I reflected over what he had been telling me "Pat, I have no one, but you. You are the only one who understands me. I love you, Pat." As I persisted, Pastor would become irritable at my comments regarding my departure from our relationship. I would sometimes cry and he would simply retort,... "The next time I get a girlfriend, she is not going to be in the church. You keep whining about what God is thinking. God loves you, Pat. He loves me.... He understands!" I even remember responding, "The next time? You mean you would do this again?" He responded with a sarcastic chuckle and then told me he was unhappy with his wife and he needed someone that he could love. Consequently, our conversations always ended with how much he needed me and that he couldn't bear to lose me.

As I sat there and thought about my destructive situation...I finally surmised that I must be strong and courageous. I convinced myself to quit talking about all that I needed to do and to start acting on what I knew was right. In spite of my positive self-talk, I felt like I was in quicksand, the more I struggled to get out, the deeper I sunk. If you have ever been in a situation where you feel all alone and hopeless, the enemy will try to capitalize on your despair. In times of despair, it is easy to feel that God cannot be reached and that He does not hear you because of the great sin in your life. But I can assuredly tell you that God does see your struggles and He hears your inward cries for help. There can be a point in life when circumstances seem so overwhelming and we may feel totally alone without one person who understands. The self-imposed pressures caused by wrong decisions can seemingly dictate our destiny...unless God intervenes. He has a purpose and a plan for our lives that He wants to fulfill. So He stands ready at the opportunity to come to our rescue. He waits patiently on us to call Him, to acknowledge our need for Him in our life. If you so much as whimper and call His name with the weakest of tones, God hears, and He is moved with compassion. That night after the Pastor's wife had left my home, I whimpered. I was overcome with shame and had reached my lowest ebb in life. My soul yearned to be free, my spirit yearned to be under the shadow of the Almighty, and I yearned for a place of refuge from the storm. I needed a hiding place, I needed my Heavenly Father.

Should the Pastor's wife ever read this book, hopefully she will recognize the familiarity of this story and know that it is I, Patricia, who writes.

To her I say, **I am deeply sorry for the pain and the hurt I brought into your life.** I know such words as "sorry" must seem so shallow in light of the agony you had to endure. Please know that for 12 years I walked under a veil of shame. I punished myself over and over again for the hurt that I caused you and for the pain that I saw in your eyes. For years, my past failure played in auto-reverse as a constant nagging memory. I ask that you find it in your heart to forgive me, if you have not already. I desire to personally apologize to you for the needless pain you bore as a result of my thoughtless actions. But I dare not presume that such an occurrence would be welcomed by you. I hurt you immensely and I betrayed your trust. I will never forget your courage and the humility it must have taken to come to my house in search of your husband that night.

May this apology I humbly extend to you be accepted. May it add peace and not sorrow, closure and not an open door for the enemy. I desire your forgiveness and your prayers as I seek to help other women walk out of their individual prisons of shame. I believe God will use my testimony to bring restoration and restitution to many readers-to the woman whose head is hung down; to the Pastor who has walked in this Pastor's shoes; and to the Pastor's wife who has endured the hardship and the pain of betrayal. In sincere repentance I have gone to the Father and reckoned with him regarding my iniquity and He has forgiven me. His blood redeemed me and brought purity to my life.

From the standpoint of restitution and restoration, the enemy <u>will</u> pay for the damages: He will observe women nationally and internationally walk out of their chains of bondage. His plan to thwart the call of God on their lives by holding them captive to their shame will be used against Him as women declare their freedom through their voiced testimonies. Thus, their declarations will release other women to be free. It will become a contagious act of courage as women determine in their spirits they will not continue in the path of the castdown, but rather, the uplifted and they will boldly tell their story. Women will walk under a veil of glory through the channeling of God's everlasting mercy, and restoration will be imminent for the fallen man and woman. I believe these things to be so by the power of God.

God bless you and keep you in His peace.

Patricia Harris

THE MEETING

*You knocked on my door and I let you in.
You knew at my house your husband had been.
My heart was heavy and filled with shame.
You questioned my motives and I denied the same*

*You sat at my table, across from me
As I gazed at you in stark disbelief,
Here you sat, my Pastor's wife,
Whom I had known several years of my life*

*Your eyes so sad, your posture bent and worn
Your heaviness apparent, your look, forlorn
Dear God, I silently cried, "What have I done?"
To my very own home this woman has come....*

*In search of her husband, in search of her spouse
Who just seconds before, left my bed, my house
My answers to your questions were vague, full of lies
Outwardly I endured, yet inwardly I cried*

*You were betrayed by him and then by me
I was a part of the web, you too, us three
And all the ones who existed before
We were soul-tied in, to the bitter core*

*You arose to leave, to exit my house
"Give this message to my spouse.
Tell him that I am looking for him"
For you knew at my home is where he had been*

*"Okay", I said as I dropped my head
(He's actually listening on the phone in bed)
I thought to myself as I looked at you,
What more could I say, what more could I do?*

Imprisoned

*That night I sat and wept out loud
Dear God, can you turn this mess around?
I need you now, please, please help me
I've got to get out, escape and be free*

*Determination took over, as I made up mind
I would tell the Pastor the very next time...
That it is over, for once and for all,
no more meetings and no more calls*

Section Two
God's Grace
(Number Five in Scripture)

Imprisoned

CHAPTER 5
THE QUANDARY

I had previously written about Pastor and our affair to my older sister, Sherrie. I had been in possession of her letter for a week or so. As I read over it, her concern over the situation reflected urgency. She insisted that I leave immediately, without hesitation. She told me that I must find another church. After reading her letter, I was even more convinced that I had to leave.

It had only been a few days since Pastor's wife had visited my home. I was trying to plan an escape and I rehearsed what I would say. This Pastor was so persuasive and I was afraid he would talk me into staying. I kept telling myself to be strong and stick to my commitment to leave. When the Pastor stopped by after work, I told him that I had to leave, that I could no longer deal with our illicit relationship. I told him that the confrontation with his wife was more than I could bear and that I was utterly ashamed.

The pastor began to sob. He got on his knees, held my hands, and begged me not to leave. He literally cried and cried. He told me he would have no one if I left. He kept telling me that he needed me and to please not leave him. I argued with him and told him he was unfair to me. I told him I needed to get my life right with God again. He asked me where would I go and I told him I had heard of a church that was in another city.... I told him I would go there. "No, no, don't leave me" he cried. "Please let me go!" I cried back. "I love you, Pat," he said. "I need you. Please don't leave me, I have no one else but you." Pierced by his outcries of helplessness, I relented and stayed.

It seemed like eternity had gone by since that day I made the decision to stay. Time slowly passed until our affair reached the fourth month. It felt like it had been four years of my life. Each day was long and burdensome. Sadness and despondency became my constant companions. How I wanted to be free and make a fresh start. I moved into a new apartment and my mother flew in from out of state to assist me with the unpacking.

Since my mother was an ordained evangelist, Pastor invited her to speak at his church. My mother knew Pastor and his wife on an acquaintance basis. Initially, Mom had met Pastor when she had visited my former husband, Fred and I, several years earlier. At that time, Pastor oversaw another congregation in another city in which we all resided. On one other occasion, Pastor had also visited my parents at their home.

Unaware of our affair, Mom accepted Pastor's invitation to preach at his church. Her message, "I am satisfied with Jesus, but is Jesus satisfied with me?" ripped at my soul. I was utterly ashamed and embarrassed. By now there were whispers at the church that I was involved with the Pastor. And here stood my own mother who preached a message that tore through to the core of my very being. I wanted desperately to yell out "No, Jesus is not satisfied with me! " I sat in the back of the church and wept as she preached. I did not want anyone to look at me or to focus in my direction. I was drowning and there was no apparent lifeline, no one who could help me.

I had no established relationships with any of the ladies from church. The one with whom I felt the closest was still far too distant for me to confide in for help. Though the pastor and I had never been caught in the act ... the word was out ... we were clearly under suspicion.

I desperately needed a lifeline.... I was drowning. My life was literally dangling. I felt hopeless. I wanted to tell my mother, but how could I bring myself to mouth such a sordid confession. I struggled with telling her, but every time I got the courage, I would change my mind.

During the two weeks my mother visited me, the Pastor stopped by only once "to see my mother" so it appeared. He did not call me or request a meeting. During this time, I prayed and asked God for help to leave him. I got up enough courage to tell my mother that I was "infatuated" with the Pastor. I asked her to pray for me. She did. She hugged me and told me that I was just lonely and assured me that God had someone special for me. She didn't scowl at me for the "infatuation story" at all. I almost felt I could tell her the truth, but then, I changed my mind. Mom departed to return home. I was left alone again.

The Pastor called later on that day to tell me he was coming over. My kids were in day care and I did not have any classes or work that day (I was a full-time college student and a part-time employee). I told him on the phone that I wanted to end it and not to come over. He insisted... "I'm coming over". He was at my door within the hour. Again, another encounter took place. I cried, "I can't go on like this. My mother just preached a message about whether God was satisfied with me." "He's not," I told Pastor. He refused to listen and kept reminding me of his need for me.

He eventually left. I sat in my bedroom which had now become a "defiled den of iniquity". This was his first time alone with me in my new apartment since I had moved in. I had wanted to keep the environment pure...but now the evil spirits were running rampant in my new apartment.

I began to cry like never before. I sobbed and sobbed before the Lord. Help me! I cried out! This is bigger than me and I do not have the power to fight it. Satan was holding me in captivity. He knew I was too weak to stand up to the Pastor. Only God could break the chains of Satan's control in my life.

Everything within me was crushed. I felt I was literally on the brink of falling apart. My heart was broken, my spirit was limp, I was barely hanging on. My body, soul and spirit, though defiled, were desperately pleading for mercy. I gasped as though my heart would break as I fell on my knees and face, and came before His mercy seat. With everything within me, I desperately cried out for help!

Over and over again I asked for God's forgiveness. I had sinned against Him, the Body of Christ, my family and myself. The shame of my sins were before me and upon me. I repented and repented and repented and cried and wailed. I cried so hard my stomach ached. Then, suddenly, as if I had been given a tranquilizer, I fell into a deep, deep sleep for about two hours. When I awoke, all I could remember was dreaming about angels walking around me. I sat there for a few minutes as I gathered my thoughts. I then glanced at my watch. I was startled at the time. I had to rush to get my children from day care.

Just as I was rushing to leave, the phone rang. It was Pastor. Suddenly, a new courage and strength rose up in me... and without wincing or batting an eye, I told him it was over! I would never be back to his church! I told him I had been forgiven and that I was going to get back on the right track with God. I informed him that I would be joining another church in another city. He then did the usual begging and crying for me to stay. I made it clear once again that it was over, I then hung up on him. The phone rang again. It was him. I hung up. The phone rang several times and I picked it up and immediately hung it up again. It felt good to finally put the devil under my feet. He had been riding my back too long... and I was glad I was finally kicking His butt. I no longer felt any emotional ties for Pastor whatsoever. It was absolutely amazing! A complete transformation had taken place while I slept. I had an inexplicable strength that was supernaturally imparted. I wasn't going to change my mind! God had broken the chains and set me free!

I believe in my spirit that while I slept the angels I dreamed of were actually dispatched by God to fight the battle I could not fight. They destroyed the enemy and overtook the powers of darkness. My Father in heaven heard my cry and He delivered me! I was freed from the stronghold of Satan and His dominion and control in my life. His grip had been broken! I was coming home to God. All my heavy burdens were noticeably gone. I was happy and free as I departed to pick up my children.

GOD CAME AND RESCUED ME

I'm satisfied with Jesus, but is Jesus satisfied with me?
No, He isn't, I thought as my mother preached the message.
If she only knew the truth, what would she say?
I would break her heart if I told her…. I am so ashamed.

The battle raged and railed within my soul
I was so weak, no will to fight, no ability to win
I succumbed to evil, to the situation at hand
Though void of peace, I continued to sin

I had forsaken my God, my life seemingly doomed
A mistress at will, driven by sinful lusts and wanton pleasures
I guess I belonged to Pastor now
No one else would care, understand or be there to help me

No one listens, instead, they whisper about me
My own decisions had resulted in the mess I was in
Now, the grass is no longer green, the birds do not sing
Instead, blackness engulfs me. Where can I go? What can I do?

Evil invades my home, resides in my room.
Leave me alone, I cry. Please go away.
I felt defenseless, I was so weak….
All I had was prayer, one last desperate prayer

And so I prayed. From my inner most being I cried out
God help me! I am drowning! I'm going under!
Help me, please. I want out, I want to be free!
The heavens rumbled back, God heard me! And He came!

I didn't actually see them, but I know that Angels were there
They fought for me and destroyed every demon that had prevailed
They whipped those demons at the command of God's Word
They were smacked around, then slaughtered as they cried for mercy

Then the final command came to crush their heads
"We'll let Patricia do that when she awakens," He said
God gently reached down, lifted my sleepy head and I awoke.

The phone rang, it was Pastor… I crushed their heads with the heel of
my foot and then I hung up. "I'm free" I said "at last!"

CHAPTER 6
THE PRODIGAL DAUGHTER

I will never forget the day I walked into this crowded church. I had never seen such a boisterous display of jubilant worship. People unashamedly stood in the foyer of this church and boldly prayed. On one side, I saw men holding hands with men, and women with women. In another corner, I saw two women and one man hold hands and pray. At the other end, I saw a man and a woman pray for one another. Rejoicing, people cried to each other "be blessed" and "God is awesome."

In a daze, I slowly absorbed this unabashed, unpretentious scene as I walked around the corner into the sanctuary. There, I found a seat in the back of the packed sanctuary with my two little children. It had been one week since I had broken all ties with Pastor.

How I yearned to be in the presence of the Lord where no one looked at me or scorned me. Though a bit overwhelming, it felt so good to be in this church. I sensed such love and authenticity among these people. They sang songs with an oom-pah, Jewish beat.

I had never heard songs like these before. In the front of the sanctuary, identically dressed ladies with ribbons tied to their tambourines skillfully waved their instruments with exhilaration and unbridled joy.

There were so many young people in this church my age. There were as many men as there were women. I found that to be quite unusual. These young people earnestly danced before the Lord with all their might. I knew I had found my home. This was where I would take refuge from the storm and begin my healing. And, oh, how I wanted to be healed of the huge, gaping scars that I bore, yet no one else could see. I knew if there were ever a place to begin my healing, it was this church, Christian House of Prayer (C.H.O.P.). I had heard good things about the pastor and his wife and how they really loved God and His people. I did not know the pastor's name yet but I was so excited to be in the midst of this great congregation. I was overwhelmingly grateful to God for directing me here.

After a time of heartfelt worship, the pastor rose to speak. He was one of the most radiant men I had ever seen. He smiled and greeted the people with a hearty "Amen" and "Praises to God". (I turned to the person next to me and asked for the name of the pastor and they told me "His name is Pastor Nate Holcomb and his wife is Pastor Valerie.") (During the writing of this book I discovered that Pastor Holcomb is now a Bishop - a promotion from God)!

Pastor Holcomb began to lead the church in a confession of faith that went something like this: "People are standing in line to get in this church to hear the Word of God. For this is a prosperous year for us and the doors of success have been opened. We shall succeed in everything through Christ. The door of failure has been closed and we shall not know defeat." They repeated this three times and then they closed with Romans 4:21: "And being fully persuaded, that what He had promised, He is able also to perform."

Oh, how desperately I wanted to confess what they were saying. I wanted to confess that I would not know defeat any more in my life. I was going to learn that confession, I thought to myself. I felt like I was in heaven. Thank you, God, for sending me here! These people really believe in you, Lord! I believe they must really love you.

Then I heard the pastor say at the conclusion of his message, "Maybe we have a prodigal daughter or a prodigal son who wants to come home. This is your day. Don't put it off any longer."

"...You knew the Lord but you turned your back on Him," he continued. "You left home and ended up in the pigpen of life, but you've come to your senses and now you want to come home. Your Father is waiting for you. He wants to put a ring on your finger and throw a robe around you as He welcomes you home. He's preparing a celebration for your homecoming. Are you ready to come home?"

By this time, I was crying so hard, I couldn't see. My little girl kept asking me if I was okay. "Yes, sweetie, I'm fine," I told her through tear stained eyes. Amidst the heart-wrenching sobs, I got up and went down the aisle to the front of the church. I honestly don't know if anyone else answered the altar call that day because as far as I knew, it was just me and the Lord. I had come home!

I actually sensed that He was waiting for me, to place a robe around me and a ring on my finger. And what a glorious homecoming He had arranged for me at the altar that Sunday morning. "I'll never leave you again Father, I will never leave you again," I cried out, my arms extended to the heavens as hot tears of joy streamed down my cheeks. "I'm home, dear Father—I'm finally home!"

As Pastor Holcomb prayed for me and others gathered and laid hands on me, the Lord met me that day at the altar. I was gloriously baptized with the Holy Spirit. I literally felt my Father's arms around me. He held me like a baby as I cried and rejoiced.

"I'm home and I am free!" I proclaimed. I felt like Martin Luther King, Jr., that day. "Free at last, free at last, thank God Almighty, I am free at last!"

THE PRODIGALS' HEART

Like a husband He was to me, looking after my cares, my needs
His provision in my life was seen, By faith I walked, in Him believed
But as the world turned, so did I, for I departed and left His side
I sought to fill my flesh with sin—absorbed it all and took it in

While on my journey, life seemed unfair, I was so lonely, and in despair
Where was the joy I had known before? The peace? The grace? and so much more?
Would He be happy if I came home? I miss Him, I miss Him, I'm so alone.
He always promised that He'd be there, no matter what, no matter where

I journeyed home in hopes to see, That, like a husband, He'd be waiting for me
As I crossed the horizon, there He stood, Waiting for my arrival as I'd hoped He would
As our eyes met, the tears came too, The faster we ran, the closer we drew
He picked me up and spun me around, And on my head He placed a crown

"My princess, you have come home to Me, I missed your face, your praise, your glee"
He loved on me and held me close, I loved Him so, but He loved me most
What grace, what mercy He had for me, No questions asked, no wavering
He took me back just as I was, And gave me His unbridled love

In His presence I belonged, He embraced me as I had never known
"Welcome home" He whispered to me, "I stood in the gap so this could be"
"And now you're home, don't ever leave, for in Me lies your destiny"
I kneeled on the ground and washed His feet, I wept at His throne, His mercy seat

My alabaster box was at my side, He knew my thoughts and he wiped my eyes
As I reached to get it, He touched my hand, "you are forgiven Patricia Ann"
What manner of love could this be, that He would say such things to me?
His love so pure, His commitment strong, forever with Him I belonged

"From this day forth will you be My bride?" He asked of me with tears in His eyes,
"I will" I said as I looked at Him, I'll never leave from your side again
Then on my finger He placed His ring, the most gorgeous one I'd ever seen.
And on my shoulder He placed His robe, and to each other we were betrothed

CHAPTER 7
HE GAVE ME A NEW NAME

With every passing Bible study, praise and worship service or fellowship gathering, God knitted my heart closer to my new church family. My life began to take on a new meaning. My children made new friends and I experienced restoration, joy and peace. At long last, life took on new purpose and significance as I pursued my college studies while working in an EEO Office branch of Civil Service. My boss, a strong, vibrant woman of Baptist background, staunchly believed it important to reach down and help others achieve and she lived it in her everyday actions.

My boss came into my office early one morning and told me that a city pageant was to be held and that she would like me to become a contestant. She said the participants would be judged on talent, creativity, appearance, fitness and personality. I explained to her that I possessed none of the above.

She encouraged me however, "I will teach you how to do a dramatization," she replied, undaunted. She introduced me to the works of James Weldon Johnson and his great poetic piece entitled *The Creation*. This eloquent prose described the creation of man by God. She instructed me to memorize the words. She would then work with me at the end of each day and teach me the dramatic gestures.

Unable to find any more excuses, I entered the contest. A friend agreed to watch my children for a few days after work so I could make the practices. I practiced every night at home on the "The Creation" until I knew every word and every move without thinking or blinking an eye.

One day, while at work, a young lady named Joann, who also attended Christian House of Prayer, came in to interview for a position at the EEO Office. She was offered the job and began working shortly thereafter. I shared with Joann my excitement about the upcoming pageant. I told her that one of the pageant requirements was that each participant have a male escort. I explained that I had no one to ask. She emphatically stated "I know just the guy." She said that he was single and good looking. "He is very nice, I bet he would be glad to escort you," Joann said. I asked her if she would inquire of him. Joann said she would. The next day at work she told me he said he would be glad to escort me. I was scheduled to meet him at church on Wednesday before service. I was told he was a musician and would be involved in a pre-service rehearsal. "Look for the guy on the drums, Joann said. "His name is **Eddie Harris**."

I met Eddie on that Wednesday night. Though we only had a brief introduction, I knew he was a kind man with a gentle nature. He was well groomed and pleasant; his demeanor was that of a gentleman. Inwardly, I thanked God that Joann had thought of Eddie to be my escort.

During each rehearsal, Eddie would come at the appointed time for his part in the pageant and would leave directly afterwards. Eddie was the perfect gentleman. At the close of each practice, Eddie said a few encouraging words and told me he would see me at the next rehearsal. He carried himself in a manner without question. Eddie never flirted and treated me with the utmost respect. I liked his qualities, they were rare to me, yet authentic. I remember wistfully thinking "perhaps, he will ask me out to ice cream or for a burger one of these evenings after rehearsal". But he never did, and I never insinuated my interest in him. I had made up my mind that God would go before me in all that I did and said. But I expressed to God, "I like Eddie...very much."

The night of the pageant came and Eddie was right there by my side. He escorted me on my walk as they introduced me. I was so nervous! But Eddie told me that it would be okay and he continued to encourage me through each phase of the pageant.

Before I knew it, it was time for the contestants to perform in the talent competition. Eddie said a prayer and assured me that I would do fine. He was right. I received a standing ovation that lasted for what seemed like forever. The audience so enthusiastically thundered their applause that I was both speechless and overwhelmed. It was unbelievable! Though I had never performed a dramatic presentation before in my life, that night God anointed my talent. As I stood there, the continuous applause from the audience made me feel like a million dollars.

It was finally time to call the top five runner-ups. My name was called along with the other four. I was so excited! From this point, the pageant progressed to the awards for the various segments. I can still remember the awards as if it were yesterday. They were:

Category 1: *Most Creative* (This segment consisted of a self-written narrative by each contestant, describing their goals and daily lifestyles. This narrative was read by each contestant in-turn, as the other walked and modeled their sports outfit).

Category 2: *Most Talented* (Consisted of a selected talent presented for competition)

Category 3: *Ms. Congeniality* (self-explanatory)

Crowning: *Ms. Princess* (The selected princess for the 1987 Pageant)

The spokesperson called out...."And the *Most Creative Award* goes to ... Patricia Weaver. Eddie, who was standing next to me on-stage, winked at me as I went out to accept my trophy. Again, I received a standing ovation.

The pageants emcee then turned again to face the audience and continued..."And the *Most Talented Award* goes to ... Patricia Weaver! I looked up at Eddie and again he beamed with genuine happiness at my unforeseen double blessing. I stepped out once more to accept the award, my heart bursting with joy. That night, I truly felt as if I was a recipient of two Grammies.

The *Ms. Congeniality Award* was then awarded to one of the most amiable young ladies among the contestants.

As the emcee came to the conclusion of the evening's festivities, Eddie looked at me and said, "I believe it is you, I believe you are going to win the crown." Shortly after he said those words, the pageant host paused for a moment and then, with the card identifying the winner in her hand, she spoke in a high, resonant voice that pierced the hushed auditorium: "Our 1st runner up is... (when she didn't call my name I knew I had won the title). And our *New Princess for 1987* is..................Ms. Patricia Weaver!

"Oh, my God," I thought in wide-eyed disbelief and shock. Can this be true? I thought numbly as I walked to the front and center and received my beautiful, silver rhinestone tiara, a satin sash and bouquet of roses. That night, I was crowned a "Princess" before hundreds of people who applauded my success. As the music played, I walked onto the runway with Eddie, my escort, by my side, waving through tearful eyes to the cheering crowd. Eddie then stood aside and let me walk alone. As I took my victory walk, though outwardly smiling and waving at the well-wishers, I inwardly thought about where I had come from just a few months ago. In that not too distant past, I had wallowed in the pig pen ... but tonight, ... I had been given a new name, a new identity and a crown, all because of

God's awesome love. I deserved nothing, yet He gave me everything. He wanted me to know that He saw me as His princess.

I am reminded of a woman who was crowned a national princess many years ago. Shortly after her victory it was discovered that her past consisted of questionable behavior which did not bring honor to the crown. This precious soul was stripped of her glory and the accolades. The media discredited her and cast "shame" upon her. No longer was she viewed a "princess " in their eyes. They took her crown away for failure to meet pageant criteria. She was perceived as "unworthy" to be a princess according to the "rules".

Yet, here I stood, amongst resounding applause, the least of all. Every woman in the pageant was "worthier" than I. My past was made plain before God, He knew my failures, my track record of impurity...and yet, He crowned me a "princess". This pageant, was a man-made event, but God was the ultimate judge. Just as God chose David, who was out in the field tending the sheep and considered least of all, ...He also chose me. I was the least likely to be worthy of a crown, yet God, who knew my unspeakable failures, and the "shame" of my past, viewed me as <u>His</u> princess. He bypassed the "rules" and counted me worthy. He pronounced me a "princess" and gave me a "crown".

My Father God knew how little I thought of myself and how I struggled with personal shame. So, in His own special way, He lifted my chin and held my head up. In His eyes I was somebody special. I was not rejected but was acceptable in the beloved through Christ Jesus.

"Thank you, sweet Jesus", I said, as I continued to wave to the cheering crowd and walk the length of the stage. I completed my walk and went back to stand beside Eddie, he looked at me and said what my own heart was feeling, "Praise God!"

THE PRINCESS

How could I be a princess, with a crown, awards and gifts?
I feel so unworthy
Yet God said, "I count you worthy,
My ways are past finding out."

"As far as the east is from the west so are your sins from Me", He said.
"I have cast them into the sea of forgetfulness to remember them no more.
I will have mercy upon whom I will have mercy.
Though your sins be as scarlet, I will wash them whiter than snow.
Come to the mercy seat, where you will experience
My grace, My love"

"For I am great and greatly to be praised, for I alone reign.
My purpose will always prevail.
All have fallen short of my Glory.
Yet, all can obtain right standing because of My Grace,
because of the redemptive blood of Jesus"

"Tell them that "I AM" crowned you and made you a princess."

CHAPTER 8
MY KNIGHT IN SHINING ARMOR

As the newly crowned City Princess, I was scheduled to make guest appearances at luncheons, banquets, modeling shows, churches, breakfasts, recreation centers and wherever they could send me. I was asked to perform "The Creation" for about 90% of my guest appearances. My escort, Eddie, was asked by the pageant officials to be present at every appearance to serve as my chaperone. Eddie kindly acquiesced, freely volunteering his services. To me, I felt he was a chaperone sent by God Himself.

After one month of guest appearances, the friendship between Eddie and I began to blossom. As our interest in one another developed into a romantic attraction, Eddie asked me out on a date. We went bowling and took my children on our first date. The following week we went on a picnic with the children as well. And on our third date we went to a drive-in movie with my two little buddies in tow. After these three dates, Eddie felt that the Lord told him that I was to be his wife. He asked me to marry him. My mouth almost fell open. I didn't expect a proposal from Eddie. I had never experienced such genuine love, gentleness and kindness as shown by this man. We had only dated three times and known each other for just over a few months. Despite this, I knew Eddie was genuine and sincere, totally different than any man I had ever known. When I was with Eddie, I forgot my sordid past. It was as if I had crossed over into another world—an innocent, pure world.

I said "Yes" to his proposal without even thinking about all that I needed to disclose to him. I was so excited and happy ... "yes, yes, yes" was all I could think and say.

Within a week, the Lord impressed upon my heart to share my past with Eddie. Deep within, I had been agonizing over how to share it with him. I just didn't know what to expect. I was fearful of losing Eddie, yet I knew he had to know the truth about me and my past. The Word from the Lord was to tell him soon without delay. I submitted to God's direction. Inwardly I wrestled on how to share my deepest, darkest secrets with Eddie. Should I tell him I had genital herpes first or would I first tell him about my affair with Pastor? How awful it was going to be. I could only imagine the worst. I cried because I knew my past was who I was and I could not run away from the truth. It had been almost a year since the beginning of the affair with the Pastor. The painful memories were still there. I knew I had been forgiven, yet the shame from my past was overwhelming.

The following Sunday, Eddie invited the kids and me over for dinner at his apartment after church. He was a very good cook and had prepared a delicious meal for us. After we ate, the kids laid down for an evening nap. I then told Eddie that I needed to discuss something with him. We stepped out into a field across from his apartments. I could see the balcony door of Eddie's apartment from the field where I stood. He left it open so we could hear the kids if they awakened. It was warm that evening and I remember seeing the stars twinkle brightly as nightfall rapidly approached.

Though I had now acquired a new name as a princess, and many of the local townspeople referred to me by this title, I also had a past from which I could not escape. I felt I would always be haunted by the stigma of my illicit relationship with Pastor for the rest of my life. I knew Eddie wanted and deserved a precious jewel for a wife, a woman of virtue. He deserved to have such and I knew I was tainted. As I attempted to tell Eddie, I could not control the tears. In fact, I could barely speak.

My Knight in Shining Armor 47

Patiently, Eddie held me close and continued to tenderly inquire about what was bothering me. Finally, he gently urged, "Just say it, Patricia." I knew there was no easy way to say it. With all the courage I had, I relayed to Eddie about the herpes first (the lesser of two evils in my opinion). I explained how it had come about in my previous marriage. He looked at me and said "Is that it?" (Is that it? I couldn't believe my ears. He didn't wince or grimace when I told him about my incurable sexually transmitted disease.) He told me we would both deal with it together and make the best of the situation. Eddie assured me that herpes would not prevent us from getting married nor did it change his love for me.

I told him there was more that I needed to share. As I looked into his eyes with tears pouring down my cheeks, I confessed to this dear, unassuming young man that I had a four-month affair with my previous pastor. I told him the name of the pastor. Eddie quietly acknowledged that he knew him. Eddie then looked at me with the most sincere eyes, he held my chin in his hands and he unflinchingly stated:

"If God has forgiven you, then so do I, Patricia, and you know that God has forgiven you. I love you and I want you to be my wife," he said. The matter was settled.

Then out of the clear blue, Eddie picked me up and swung me around so as to lift my spirits and make me smile, (it worked – I smiled). He then stopped and held me like a baby with my head against his chest and my 98-pound frame in his arms. He looked at me eye-to-eye and reassured me that we were supposed to be together. He said, "I love you, Patricia Harris". (He called me by his last name as a confirmation of his commitment to me, his bride-to be.) He then put me down and hugged me like I was a china doll. We walked back to his apartment hand in hand. Tears of joy were streaming down my cheeks for I knew

God had given me the man of my dreams. The man I could share my hopes with, who would understand my needs and who would always be there. God had selected Eddie to be my husband and me, his wife.

As I look back on that night, I now realize that Eddie represented a type and shadow of God's unconditional love and His boundless mercy. God calls us by His name no matter what our past may be. He picks us up and holds us like a baby, reassuring us of His love as He reminds us that we are His bride-to-be.

A few weeks after I disclosed my past to Eddie, he received a letter from a friend of his who told him that she had heard a rumor about me and felt he should know. This older lady was a dear friend and was only addressing the issue out of concern. She wanted to ensure that Eddie was aware of any possibly hidden secrets. I believe her heart was pure and she was only looking out for his best interest. Eddie called this lady friend and informed her that we had already addressed the personal issues of my past and he assured her that he knew, without a doubt, I was the woman for him. I was so glad I listened to the Lord about disclosing my past without delay. God knew that Eddie was soon to find out and He wanted it to come from me first, before Eddie heard it from another.

Several ladies in the church whom I had come to know told me that Eddie had been at the church for two plus years and that he was considered a "possible husband" for some of the single sisters. In other words, some of the young ladies were "naming and claiming," I guess. He was such a gentleman, very regal. I can certainly see why he was an eligible bachelor. Yet, God had reserved Eddie for me. He was my special blessing.

Three months after Eddie's proposal, we married. Eddie and I did not consummate our union until our wedding night. I was so happy! I was on the right path in life. I had overcome some odds in my life, and finally I could see the light at the end of the tunnel. I had a godly man for a husband, a man who really loved and cherished me. Someone with whom I could share my dreams and secret ambitions. Someone who believed in me. I loved my husband, I knew I would always love him and be a faithful wife. Eddie had a heart of gold - he was a "real" man.

THE KNIGHT IN SHINING ARMOR & HIS PRINCESS

*As a young woman, I would dream of your might
that you were a strong, valiant, warring knight
Upon your stallion you would ride into town
and everyone far and near would come around*

*All the girls dressed so pretty to catch your eye
in hopes their looks would be their bribe
You were such a charming gentleman
and would say kind words to all of 'em.*

*But in your search, you continued your stride
for you were looking for a special bride
Not just any girl could be your wife
she had to be one fit for a knight*

*A "girl" with a perfect past was not the "girl" of your dreams
you sought for one who offered more it seems
The woman you wanted would have to "love" you
she would have to adore you, be faithful and true*

*All her troubles would not dismay
the love you had to give away
You knew some day you would see her face
her shyness, her smile, and her grace*

*And then one day, there she stood
strolling through your neighborhood
She looked so frail, yet so sweet
you knew this girl you had to meet*

*And like a gentleman, you offered her a ride
upon your stallion, to sit by your side
She gazed at you, as you looked at her
could she be the answer to your prayer?*

My Knight in Shining Armor

*And so you spent time with this charming girl
you noticed her smile, her eyes, her curls
She had found a place in your heart
you couldn't leave her, or be apart*

*And then one night she confessed to you
her hurts, her past, and all of her wounds
You wiped her tears and dried her eyes
and told her, she's the one, she's the bride*

*(The young girl speaks):
"When I was young I dreamt of you
I never thought it would come true
Throughout my life I asked God for a man,
who would be true and understand,*

*That I've fallen short, and I've made mistakes
and sometimes I've fallen flat on my face,
Could one accept me just as I am?????
I've asked God, ... if there is such a man."*

*(The Knight speaks:) "I am he, I am the one
I understand from where you've come
And I forgive you for your past
come on let's celebrate our love at last ...!"*

*And so came their wedding to honor their life
for finally he had ended the search for his wife
And on the stallion, they rode off in happiness
the Knight in shining armor and his beautiful princess*

CHAPTER 9
GOD'S AMAZING GRACE

In pursuit of Eddie's dream to play the drums professionally, we moved to Dallas two months after we were married. Due to the unanticipated move, I relinquished my crown as City Princess. So, in a formal ceremony, I passed the title on to the first runner up. However, I knew in God's eyes and in Eddie's I would always be a princess. God had used the pageant to serve its purpose in my life and I was content to move on. In the midst of this transition, I also discovered in our third month of marriage that I was pregnant. I was approximately four weeks along at the time we found out. Eddie was to become a first time birth father.

At this point in our lives, all was going well. We both were adjusting to married life, Eddie for the first time and me for the second. As they say, the first year is always the toughest. Due to the fact that our courtship was only three months in duration, Eddie and I learned about each other's peculiarities after we were married. We both were determined to adjust, and so we did. But to add to our period of adjustment, my herpes flared up for the third time in our less than one-year marriage. I was in my seventh month of pregnancy during the third flare-up. The doctor told me that if the herpes remained active at the time of the baby's delivery, I would have to undergo a caesarian section for the baby's protection.

Eddie never became upset about the herpes. He never seemed annoyed, and never said a critical or cruel word to me regarding it. He refused to hurt or reject me in any way. Eddie was true to his word. He said we would make the necessary adjustments and we did. He was as calm about the herpes at the time of the flare-ups as he was the night I confessed to him in the field by his apartment.

As the delivery day approached, Eddie and I discussed names for our new baby. I told Eddie that I was confident she was a girl. One day, while at home cleaning, I paused and began to search the TV channels. I finally decided to stop momentarily at a channel that featured a talk show. As I continued my household cleaning, I suddenly heard the talk show host exclaim in astonishment.... "Amazing Grace!" At that same moment, I heard the Lord speak to my spirit and say, "Her name will be Amazing Grace." When Eddie came home from work, I told him what the Lord had said, but he had few words, if any, regarding the name (after all, "Amazing Grace" wasn't a name you would normally choose for your child).

So I asked God for a second confirmation, just so we could be sure. I felt, as Eddie himself admitted to me, that "Amazing Grace" was a very odd name for a child. One night, while the kids were in bed, and Eddie at work, I was in the den folding clothes and putting them away, again, with the TV on in the background. I walked from the den to the bedroom and back again methodically putting away clothes. As I did this, I heard the ending of a TV show ... the only words that caught my attention were "Amazing Grace! Amazing Grace!" I quickly walked over to the television and observed the credits as they rolled on the screen. There was an actor's name who played the role of "Amazing Grace". In this show, Amazing Grace was a boy. I took a seat, utterly shocked. I had never heard of anyone named Amazing Grace, boy or girl. This particular show was portraying the life of a baseball player. So God answered my prayer and confirmed her name. I shared the confirmation with Eddie and he agreed that her name would be "Amazing Grace."

But why this name? I even wondered if she were going to be physically challenged ...and that perhaps her name was chosen by God because she would be an overcomer. Once during a visit with Pastor Valerie Holcomb, I told her the name of our baby. Pastor Valerie suggested we look up "amazing" in another language and use that translation for the first name, instead of just calling her "amazing". We took her suggestion and researched several foreign language books. Eddie and I both liked the Romanian translation for "Amazing" - "Amira". We chose the translation, "Amira", in lieu of calling her "Amazing". As mentioned, prior to Amira's birth, we never found out the disclosure of her sex, we just believed in our hearts she was a girl, at least I did. Eddie was pretty flexible. However, with the God given name of "Amazing Grace", he was hoping it was a girl.

In my seventh month of pregnancy, I prayed that God would heal me of herpes because of the potential risk to our baby. Eddie agreed with me in prayer as well, that God would heal me so that our little baby would not be at risk. In addition, we just wanted overall healing. Herpes is a very painful and uncomfortable venereal disease. The lesions produced by this disease can sometimes be unbearable. For a woman, it can be difficult to sit, stand or walk comfortably during active stages. I can recall intense pain for up to 3 days before it would finally subside. I accepted this disease as a punishment for my past failures. In my own lowly opinion of myself, I felt that I needed some type of permanent reminder for what I had done in my past. The herpes was indeed permanent and incurable, and thus, my reminder. Yet, Eddie didn't deserve it and though he never complained, my heart went out to him because he was exposed and at risk. Conversely, his heart and tender compassion went out to me as I suffered excruciating pain with each episode.

With Amira's delivery, the Lord blessed the herpes to be inactive. She was born vaginally and with no complications. We were proud parents of a beautiful baby girl. Her older sister and brother were elated about the addition to our family. To date, at the writing of this book, <u>it has been</u>

<u>over ten years</u> since Eddie and I prayed for God to heal me of herpes, **And He did!** We are not for sure of the exact date of my healing, but we believe He healed me while I was pregnant with Amira. My last outbreak of herpes was in the seventh month of pregnancy when we both sought God for healing. Since that time, <u>I have never had another herpes episode.</u> It's been over ten glorious years of walking in the miraculous healing of the Lord. Research states that "herpes" is an incurable disease. (Whose report will you believe? I will believe the report of the Lord! His Word says that I am healed!) Truly, God supernaturally healed me through the blood of Jesus! I never went through a prayer line, I never felt a rush of any kind go through my body. It was our mustard-seed faith and the gentle touch of God's healing power, grace and mercy that healed me. I was miraculously healed from an incurable disease! To God be the glory forever and ever!

I believe God especially honored my husband's commitment to love and cherish me, unconditionally. In my spirit I am convinced that because Eddie obeyed the voice of God, married me without wavering, and cherished me as if I were his virgin, that he won favor with God. I am convinced my husband's love for me so modeled God's love for the church, that Eddie moved the heart of God, and God was merciful and healed my diseased body. In keeping with **His Amazing Grace** ...God also protected Eddie from the transference of the disease. God is so awesome! He really <u>is all we ever need</u>.

GOD'S AMAZING GRACE

How much does it cost, what is its price?
The value of it, is more than one could pay
Could it ever be purchased with the finest in gold and silver?
Its cost would far exceed all the wealth this world could offer

Can one invest in this great commodity?
The dividends come without investment
Can one barter to acquire this great asset?
There is no equal exchange

Surely, one must do something to be a benefactor!
One must do nothing, it can not be earned
Can the most upright be given careful consideration?
It is simply an unearned merit

Are there strings attached? Loop holes perhaps?
It is simply given freely
How?
It is unmerited favor.

God's Amazing Grace, can not be earned, it is simply given
We could never be good enough, right enough or perfect enough
His amazing grace saves, it heals, it restores, it is everlasting

God is Love,
God is Amazing and full of Grace

CHAPTER 10
THE PAST RETURNS

When Amira was just two weeks old, we returned to Christian House of Prayer so Pastor Holcomb could dedicate her to the Lord. Pastor Holcomb and Pastor Valerie invited us to their home for dinner after the service.

After dinner, Pastor Valerie invited me into another room because she wanted to talk with me privately. She told me she had heard something and wanted to know if it was true. She said that she was told that I had had an affair with a certain pastor at another church. She immediately told me that she came to my defense and told the bearer of this news that I was Ms. City Princess and that they must have had the wrong person. However, they emphatically insisted that, no, I was the one. The shame, the shame that I felt was unbelievable. I began to cry and cry. "Yes, it is true" I told her. At this point, it had been almost two years since it had happened ... and I was crushed that it had come up again. I had been living with the scars and shame everyday since it happened. I silently dwelt within my own self-imposed prison of memories and chains of my past....but to hear that my past was coming up again and was still present before me was more than I felt I could bear. Pastor Valerie remained spirit-led throughout this entire disclosure. She was, of course, deeply saddened to hear that it was true, but she was also righteously indignant regarding the situation and how the enemy had taken advantage of me. She encouraged me and prayed with me. I told her that I wanted it to be behind me and that I had somehow naively, perhaps, hoped that after nearly two years, it would be. She asked if Eddie knew. "Yes, I told him before we were married. Eddie loves me so much. He said God had told him I was to be his wife. Therefore, Eddie married me in spite of my past." Pastor Valerie consoled me and loved me.

I departed with Eddie that day and told him about my conversation with Pastor Valerie. He was so hurt for me. He knew how challenged I had been in working through the issues of my past. I relayed to him how much love Pastor Valerie showed me and that she didn't judge me or scorn me. She just held me and loved me and that truly ministered to me.

The fact remained, however, that no matter what, my past was who I was. I knew that I couldn't run and I couldn't hide, but I could withdraw, so I did. I would try to be low-keyed in the church and try to maintain a low profile. God had gifted me with writing skills for plays, skits, and poetry. I decided I would use them on occasion, but not too often, because I felt I didn't deserve to be used too much by God in the church. After all, I had failed him. Consequently, I became my own judge and jury.

In the church in which I grew up, when you committed an "unpardonable transgression" you were barred from all activities, boards, and ministries and had to sit in the front pew of the church as penance. You were under scrutiny and observation until released. I felt I, too, deserved similar treatment. Since I had no one to monitor my involvement ... I monitored it myself. Sometimes I would see myself really letting go and being used in my gifts of writing or in drama. But, then I would abruptly pull back and examine what I was doing. Who do you think you are? I berated myself. If anyone knew, you wouldn't be doing anything. As a result, a cloud of shame, low self-worth, and heaviness constantly hovered over me. But I felt I deserved it. I became paranoid at the possibility of being in the presence of pastors and their wives unless I had developed a prior relationship with them before their God-ordained position. To be in close proximity to any pastor and his wife was a constant reminder of my failure.

I have never met another minister like this Pastor in the past, nor has there ever been another pastor to ever approach me in an ungodly manner. In retrospect, I now know that because I had never forgiven myself I did not feel worthy to have relationship with Pastors and their wives except on a very platonic level. Again, the enemy was at work sowing seeds of deception in my life, robbing me of my gifts, talents and anointing and ultimately postponing my destiny for as long as he could.

THE PAST RETURNS

Oh no ... could this be? Who still remembers when?
My past is ever present, my sins are lingering
Tell me it isn't so ... how I want to vanish!
There is no where to run, no where to hide

I have to accept the fact that my past is who I am!
I have been a failure! Is there no hope for me now?
Is it true once doomed, always doomed?
Can redemption help me rise again?

I have brought shame on my life, my name is ruined.
Can God redeem this wretched soul that I am?
Am I worth the time it would take to heal this broken vessel?
I am trying Lord to walk away, to live a different life.

But the past is ever present, and I am reminded of my failures.
I feel so weak, so faint, so ashamed
Father God, I need you. Do you hear me now?
I know you are there, but yet you feel so distant.

I weep before your throne, I weep and I groan
Your daughter feels the intense sorrow of her past
The enemy is all around me ... he will give me no peace.
Will the day ever come when I will arise in victory?

Oh, Father, your daughter feels the intense sorrow of her past.
I groan in agony ... the veil of shame covers me.
My pain is mine to bear. I am so burdened.
I want you to take this pain, I want to cast it upon you

But, I am so ashamed, ... I must bear this pain alone.
I feel the presence of darkness, it hovers over me.
It gives me no peace, it reminds me...
But I don't want to remember, yet my past is ever before me.

CHAPTER 11
THE UNEXPECTED

Eddie would listen to me when I would cry about my past. Of course, the biggest issue would always be Pastor. Eddie encouraged me to move forward, to give it to God once and for all. But within, I wrestled that it really wasn't God's problem. It wasn't God's fault that I carried all these weights. God had done enough for me, I reasoned. I will handle it or so I thought.

One night out of the clear blue ... the Pastor from the past called my house. Eddie answered it and the Pastor told him that his mother had died recently and he wanted me to be made aware since I knew her. Eddie, though protective of me, did not perceive any underlying motives by this call but remained cautious. He handed me the phone. (This was quite an awkward situation ... it seemed too delicate to question Pastor's motives under the circumstances. His mother had recently past away ... so I decided to give my condolences and quickly say good-bye)

I thought it was weird that he would call me. It wasn't as if his mother and I were really close (though I was sincerely sorry about her death). I guess he got our telephone number from information. I was disappointed I had heard from him.

Within a two week period Pastor called again in the evening while we were all at home. Unfortunately, I answered the phone. This time he called <u>to cry</u> about his mother's death. I felt very uncomfortable. It was obvious that he was upset and in despair about his mother. I listened and then told him Eddie and I would pray for him.

When I got off the phone, I turned to Eddie and said, "I am not sure why Pastor is calling me."

Eddie then assured me that he would talk to Pastor should he ever call again.

A month or so later I visited the Christian House of Prayer. I had gone there alone to meet with Pastor Valerie to discuss a business venture. She took me to lunch and we had a productive meeting. Just as I was preparing to leave to return home, I told her that the Pastor from my past had called me twice and the reasons for his calls. She told me, in no uncertain terms, that the next time he called, if he called, to tell him to never call me again. She said it didn't matter how sad he sounded. She expressed it was a trick of the enemy and that I had to be smarter than him. I assured her that if he called again, that I would tell him. Pastor Valerie strongly reiterated that I must be the one to tell him not to call, since it was I that Pastor sought.

Approximately a month later, Pastor did call. I was at home alone with Amira and my other two children were in school. When I answered, he sounded as calm and collected as possible, as though it were just a routine call.

"Hello Pat, and how are you?" he began. That is when I let him have it. I told him not to ever call my house again. I reiterated I was a married woman and I loved my husband and he had no right to call me. He explained that he was simply calling to say "hi." I told him that I didn't want him to call to say "hi" or call for any reason. With authority I boldly told him that I knew what he was trying to do and I assured him I wasn't interested! I angrily told him "Don't ever call me again!" While he hesitated in saying good-bye, I hung up. After hanging up, I felt assured that there were no lingering doubts in his mind that I meant what I said. I left him no room to wonder. Though somewhat shaken by this occurrence, I felt that Pastor had finally gotten the message loud and clear. How dare the enemy even think for a moment that he could destroy the new life that God had given me! That evening I told Eddie what happened and he was proud I had shown boldness in standing up to this Pastor.

Needless to say, Pastor never called my house again. However, one Sunday when Eddie and I had gone back to visit Pastor Holcomb and Pastor Valerie, after service we and our guest from Covenant Church were invited to dinner by Elder Hickson and his wife, Donna. When the church was smaller Eddie and I would sometimes eat with the Pastor and his wife when visiting. However, Pastors Nate and Valerie were not able to join us this time. The church was growing at a phenomenal rate. They had already moved into their third church building, which now had balcony seating, and they were still confessing.... "People are standing in line to get in this church to hear the word of God...." After service we all joined the Hicksons at a nearby restaurant for a delicious Sunday dinner.

Later, as we were finishing our meal, Donna, who has to be one of the wisest, most precious, spirit-led women I have ever known, discreetly leaned over to me and said.... "Pastor (his name) is right around the corner near the door where you will exit" (up until this point, I was not aware she knew of my affair with Pastor, but I'm so glad she did). She told me that his back was turned away from me and that if I kept my back away from him as I walked out, that he would probably never see me, even if he turned around. I appreciated the love with which this Elder's wife covered me. Her heart was to protect me. I leaned over and told Eddie.

As we departed, I was able to leave unnoticed and unseen by Pastor. It was hard to believe that we were both in the same restaurant. It had been almost two years since I had been back to visit this church and this city. Who would believe that this Pastor from my past would be in the same restaurant, at the same time, as me. The enemy had a plan, but it was thwarted. I was glad Donna was informed about my past. I thanked her for looking out for me. She could have questioned me for details. After all, she had just saved me from a very humiliating, embarrassing moment—perhaps I did owe her some explanation regarding my past ... but she never questioned me. She did what God told her to do and that was it. She could have looked down upon me, but instead she loved me and continued to visit with me as though this had never happened. I will never forget her kindness and her love.

THE UNEXPECTED
DEDICATED TO THE "ELDER'S WIFE"

*So as we dined, we laughed and talked
Who would have given it any thought
That in our presence this "pastor" would be
In the same restaurant with Eddie and me*

*And as we smiled and exchanged words
The subject changed and "his" name occurred
I was informed that he too was here
And in proximity he was very near*

*Therefore you told us how to leave
To keep from ever being seen
And with a plan we prepared to go
To exit out, so he would not know*

*That we had ever been inside
Eating and drinking at a table nearby
Your heart was pure, your motives divine
Your love so real, your words so kind*

*You kept me from facing yet more shame
by having to see this pastor again
So carefully we stood up to go
passing by his table, he did not know*

*that you had just led us away
by the voice of God, you had obeyed
Thank you sister, for being there
I am so glad you were aware*

CHAPTER 12
THE PRESENCE OF EVIL

Eddie and I were now in our fifth year of marriage. I was still in college. Eddie had insisted that I finish. He said he wanted me to have my Bachelor's Degree because he knew how much it meant to me. Eddie loved and cared for me in a way that was God-inspired. He protected me and watched over me like an eagle.

Though my husband is an easy-going person, there is an inner fire within him, that when empowered by the Holy Spirit can transcend into the aggressiveness of a fighting warrior. As you read on you will discover the significance of why God gave me a husband with such a mighty warring spirit.

As I unfold this chapter, I request that you ask God to mature your understanding. Ask God to give you revelatory insight into the reality of spiritual warfare so you may benefit by what I am about to share. Know this, the enemy is out to torment God's people because "we" are a threat to his (Satan's) kingdom. May God bless you to grasp the importance of knowing the defense we have against principalities and powers in high places (Ephesians 6:12).

It is my prayer that once you read this, you will be compelled to guard your purity and your relationship with God. Although I was a born-again Christian, I was still open to the attacks of the enemy and did not have the revelation on how to close the door. I didn't realize that certain parts of my soul still needed to be delivered from the soul-ties. I was still being attacked because of the open doors in my life, to include unforgiveness.

If soul ties are developed between two human beings through a spiritual transference, then it can also happen in the spirit realm with an evil embodiment. I discovered the demon sent to torment me was an incubus – a sex demon.

Satan's desire is to impact the church through whatever means necessary. An incubus desires to have a place (a dwelling) in you where he can control you in the soulish realm. Satan also desires to have your descendents, as well.

The calling card of an incubus is pornography. As you know, pornography takes place in the soulish realm ... this area can be, and is, a stronghold for many. A stronghold is indeed a "control factor" in ones' life. <u>An incubus desires to control your body, soul, and mind (spirit) – the three part being of man.</u> He is very influential. His existence can come through the bloodline as well as through soul ties. Often when coming through the bloodline, this spirit can be latent for a number of years. Once sexual impurity occurs, it can open the gateway for an incubus spirit to gain access to one's life.

The process to overcoming an evil presence is to be delivered and to come under the blood of Jesus. One must "walk" in deliverance. The enemy will always try to gain access to your life, but staying in the Word and wearing the full armor of God is the key to your success and power over Satan. Jesus was the only person who could say that Satan had no place in Him. John 14:30. Each of us however, are vulnerable to Satan's attacks. There are places in all of us where the enemy can come back and try to touch us.

The believer's deliverance can be maintained and sustained by the power of God's Word as all doors are closed to Satan. Without an open door He can't get in. He may be on the sidelines trying to intimidate, but He can't get in to touch if He has no access.

As the years passed and I continued to be judge and jury of my soul, I also became weighed down with the presence of evil spirits. As you know, in my first marriage we were both involved in extra-marital affairs. There was also my affair with the Pastor who had been bisexual in his past, which in turn opened me to all his bed partners. The accumulation of my sordid sexual past had left me with

The Presence of Evil

unsevered soul-ties as well as "open doors" for the existence of evil spirits in my life. As a matter of fact, nights were restless and fearful for me. I felt tortured at night by an evil presence, which I could feel and sense. It was horrible.

He, this evil spirit who was about eight feet tall and in silhouette form, would walk into my bedroom as Eddie and I slept. I would awaken and my body would go into a trance-like state, as if frozen and unable to move. Sometimes before entering my room, this demon would be preceded by little demonic imps with high-pitched voices. They stood about 8 inches off the ground. My body could not move at all... I could only cry out in my mind "Jesus!" It was obvious they could hear my thoughts because I would get a reaction from them; these little imps would cower at the mighty Name ... but after cowering they would continue with their antagonizing ways until, several repetitive calls on the name of Jesus, would cause them to flee. This 8-foot demon was an incubus, a sex demon from the pit of hell. I remember closing my eyes as he came and stood by my bed. (Few people understand demons, but they are on a mission. They have a plan for you if you submit, and a plan for you if you resist. They are sent to rule you, govern you and control you. However, in the midst of their control <u>God can still be reached).</u> The Lord heard my cry when I uttered "Jesus" in the spirit realm. When the incubus heard it, he had no choice but to submit to the power that is in the Name. When I initially called upon the name of Jesus, the incubus showed strong resistance by trying to choke me, smash my body against the bed and torment me with fear. I called again on the name of Jesus and this time he fled. Though this spirit had a powerful presence, he was yet too weak to withstand the power in the name of Jesus. What an awful, fearful and confusing experience. This was the first time I had encountered such. It was very foreign to me, yet, I knew it was demonic. Initially, I was too ashamed to tell my husband that a sex demon was coming into the room at night. I knew I had not invited this grotesque creature, but how could I explain its evil presence to my husband. After I had encountered the third attack I knew this incubus spirit was planning on making regular visits. Though it would flee when I called on the name of Jesus, it still kept coming back! I needed Eddie to protect me from it. I told my husband and he listened intently. Eddie was uncertain about it and felt he needed more instruction regarding the spiritual realm and how to conduct warfare. He had always tried to protect me and help me ... but this time he needed more spiritual guidance. Until he obtained direction, Eddie did all he knew to do ... pray.

We were both aware this battle was not "flesh and blood". It could only be fought in the spirit realm with the necessary weapons given by God. Eddie and I sought God for insight regarding how to effectively approach this demon who was desperately trying to rule, govern, and control my life with fear.

Somehow, we had heard of an elder in our church named Jessye Ruffin. We were told that she was involved in deliverance and spiritual warfare and had great insight in this area. However, because I was ashamed, I had planned to withhold some of the details when I met with Jessye. We made an appointment and I told her as discreetly as possible, what was happening to me. <u>She knew exactly what this demon was and what he was sent to do. I didn't have to give her any details, she discerned its roots by the Spirit.</u>

Jessye told me the demon was an incubus. (Though earlier in this chapter I referred to this demon as an incubus, I was totally unaware at the time of the actual encounters of its roots and its origin.) I told her that I was very afraid of it. She told me to pray that God would reveal its name to us so that we could directly call it out and address it in the spirit realm. Jessye also explained this demon had come as a result of an open door caused by sexual impurity in my life. She told us (Eddie and I) that we needed to break the soul-ties. (That was the first time Eddie and I had ever heard of soul-ties). She instructed Eddie on how to pray over me and told me that if I felt more comfortable with the light on at night, then to keep it on. She gave us scriptures to pray and told Eddie that he was my spiritual covering and he had authority through Christ to address those evil spirits in my behalf. Then she and her husband, Jerry Ruffin, covered us in prayer. (It has been over ten years since our initial meeting with Pastor Jessye, today she and her husband, Pastor Jerry, are the Associate Pastors of the Healing and Deliverance Ministry at Covenant Church). God used Pastor Jessye to pave the road to my eventual escape from the spiritual darkness that had encompassed me.

During this same time frame, Pastor Mike Hayes (our Pastor) requested <u>Covenant Church</u> (our church) to join him in a Daniel's Fast, (this type of fast is according to Daniel 10:2, 3. As you read on, you will see where Daniel's prayer was answered in Daniel 10: 12). For those of us at Covenant who were seeking answers and wanted to hear from God, the Daniel's fast was timely. I, along with many members in the church, went on the 21 day fast. Eddie had decided that he would go on a 40-day liquid fast consecration and refrain from all solids. My husband stands 6 feet tall, with broad shoulders and a slim physique. During this 40-day liquid fast, Eddie lost 22 pounds. His body was very lean, but his Spirit was a giant waiting for a battle to happen. The power and anointing that Eddie possessed was by the authority of the Holy Spirit.

One night in our bedroom, as I shared my fears concerning this evil presence that still kept tormenting me, my husband felt inspired to aggressively pray for me. There was a fresh power and anointing that was resident in Eddie. He laid hands on me and began to war in the Spirit for my freedom.

Eddie spent several hours in prayer and warfare and after about 3 hours, the evil presence that had seemed so overbearing was completely gone. I could feel its departure. Though I was a born-again believer and God was "Lord over my life", I realized that a part of my soul was still possessed by satan. He had been given legal rights to torment me because there were open doors in my life that had not yet been closed. I believe that all the soul ties I had ever possessed were broken off of me as God used Eddie to fight in the spirit for my sake. Thank God for my husband! God allowed him to bring deliverance to my soul as I experienced the classic signs of release. My spirit was made whole and I no longer felt fragmented. There was such an awesome presence of peace upon me as I laid down to sleep that night. I slept many, many peaceful nights thereafter.

As long as I live, I will never forget the experience I had with this demon <u>and his tormenting imps.</u> The memory of this experience makes me want to demolish Satan's Kingdom with a rage of relentless violence.

<u>Had it not been for the Grace of God, I don't know what I would have done.</u> God kept me covered through the name of Jesus.

The name of the Lord is a strong tower, the righteous run to it and they are safe. Proverbs 18:10

We are troubled on every side, yet not distressed; we are perplexed but not in despair, persecuted, but not forsaken, cast down, but not destroyed". II Corinthians 4:8,9 The Lord God reigns!

THE PRESENCE OF EVIL

I gave away the purity of my soul
In exchange for a web of soul-ties
That entangled my very being
Until I became a fraction of who I was

I consented to a lifestyle of frolic
To a lifestyle of forbidden pleasures
And in exchange I opened a door
That only deliverance could shut

And through this open door
Satan and his imps came marching in
They came to torment me
To shame me and to put fear in me

I could not comprehend
what had caused this onslaught!
Where did they come from?
Who is responsible for their presence?

Then I learned it was I. I had opened the door.
I had invited them into my life!
They had legal access to torment me!
The demons wanted my very soul!

Then I discovered how to war in the spirit,
How to prepare for battle through God's Word!
The priest of my home prepared for the battle
And through the power in Jesus' name,
He commanded them to flee, and they obeyed

That door was shut,
And legal access prohibited.
The presence of evil had to flee!

CHAPTER 13
THE LETTER

After seven years of membership at Covenant Church in Dallas, Texas, I decided to mail a letter of disclosure to my Pastors, Mike and Kathy Hayes. I did not ask for a response from them. In fact, I didn't want one. My letter was a letter of confession. I openly acknowledged to them my illicit relationship with this Pastor from my past. I felt I had to tell them. It had become such a weight on my shoulders. I told myself that it was about time they knew "who I really was." This shameful incident was forever before me and I could not get it off my mind. There was so much guilt and heaviness associated with this painful memory. I wanted all the flashbacks to just go away, but they lingered, day after day, night after night.

Even though I had been delivered from the torment of the incubus, my memory of the past was as vivid as if it had happened yesterday. It was as if I was reliving it all over again. I began to wrestle more and more with the shame of my past. I became very disappointed in myself and started feeling a sense of incompetence, unworthiness and inadequacy. I thought if I could just inform my Pastors about my past then maybe this dark heavy cloud would be lifted and I would be free of the shame. So I mailed them a brief letter as an act of "open confession".

Not the least bit daunted, Pastors Mike and Kathy continued to love me the same. It was as if they were never made aware. I was blessed by their love for me, I knew it was genuine. I never chose to personally approach them to discuss the issue because I didn't really want to. All I really wanted was to shed the weight of my hidden past. I wanted to break the invisible chains that held me captive. How I wanted to be free ... and writing that letter of confession to my pastors was a step in the right direction. However, despite this bold admission of my past guilt, I continued to silently hold on to my veil of shame because inwardly I still would not forgive myself. *One can take all the "right steps" to freedom, but if you do not let go of the pain and refuse to forgive yourself, then you have not accomplished anything by taking the "right steps." It's either all or nothing. Your motives may be good, but only Jesus can give you the grace to release it "all" to him.*

Despite the fact that Covenant Church has a growing and thriving ministry, and that Pastor Mike is dynamically anointed to teach the Word, I would not allow myself to be set free. It became a personal vendetta to forbid release of my heavy burden.

In my years as a believer I had always been challenged with reading my bible consistently. Every time I would attempt to study the bible there always seemed to be a blockage to my understanding as well as my enthusiasm for reading. However, I longed to love God's Word, I had heard others share about their growth through reading, but for me it was an arduous undertaking. The little scripture intake I did consume kept me at a notch above the enemy's strategy to destroy me. I am thankful I consumed what I did. Since I was lacking the power in my life that comes through God's Word, I consistently struggled with shame because I would not allow God's Word to cleanse me from unforgiveness. If it had not been for the grace of God, I could have easily transitioned into a depressed state of mind. Satan would always tell me the same message over and over again: "If they only knew, what would they think of you?" Though the enemy tried to destroy me with His accusations, the Holy Spirit was ever present to endow me with His mercy.

CHAPTER 14
TENSION IN THE CAMP

Time continued to pass and I graduated from college. Soon after, I started a private practice as a vocational rehabilitation counselor. I provided services to injured workers under a federal program, as well as to physically and mentally disabled clients. As my career progressed, I extended my services to the court system as a vocational expert. My degree was very versatile and I was given numerous opportunities to use it as an entrepreneur. My career had become a reality because my husband believed in me and supported me. As God anointed me with preferred contracts and allowed me to excel, my college degree and achievements became my self-worth and my career became my source of identity. I had now acquired tangible proof that I was not a total failure. I felt significant as I hid in the busyness of my growing career.

However, as time progressed, my baggage of shame became heavier and heavier. It became increasingly difficult to forgive myself. Unfortunately, I became angry toward men as a result of my unforgiveness. Sometimes I would take my anger out on Eddie and would overlook the fact he was not the one who had hurt me. Yet, I rationalized he belonged to their "tribe" ... he was a man like all the others.

Then, as if hit by a bolt of lightening, Eddie and I began to experience challenges in our marriage. The enemy was definitely at work. Satan used my harbored anger toward men as a device to bring dissension between Eddie and me (I was unaware that my final hour of redemption was drawing near, I just knew that satan was trying whatever he could to put tension between Eddie and me). The enemy started pulling tricks from every corner. Eddie and I experienced several months of tension in our marriage as we struggled to compromise and deal with the ever rising issue of ongoing conflict. It was heartbreaking to see the strong resistance we had toward each other. In short, we were experiencing a Jezebel and Ahab experience which resulted in a severe marital imbalance. The enemy was deceiving us both; it wasn't until the blinders were removed from our eyes that we could see the craftiness of Satan. He was out to destroy the most precious relationship I had ever experienced and known with a man. Our marriage is a gift from God, and Satan's plan was to bring division so he could interfere with the plan of God for our lives. However, peace entered our relationship as we submitted our will to the headship of Jesus. We sought counsel from our Elders, Wayne and Jill Blue. They prayed for us, covered us and stood with us for God's complete restoration in our marriage. Within a short period of time our relationship began to blossom and the Holy Spirit knitted our hearts together again as Eddie and I submitted our marriage to God.

TIL DEATH DO US PART

"In sickness and in health, for richer or for poorer
no matter the trials, our love would endure
we both committed "till death do us part"
those were the words we spoke from our heart

Steadfast & solid with every wind that blew
Our love was undying, and could not be moved
We held on to the vows that we had decreed
No trial or situation would change what we agreed

Then came the day when our vows were tested
Along with all the prayers we had invested
Initially we wavered in our desire to fight
There seemed to be no victory, or will to win in sight

Ahab and Jezebel stood toe to toe in us
To tolerate each other became our biggest "must"
I looked at him, and he looked at me
This Knight and His princess were now deceived

We'd turned our hearts from what was true
And forgot our vows and all "I do's"
Together we stand, divided we fall
We had lost the vision for our call

We humbled our spirits and turned to God
Together we kneeled and recalled our vows
God hearkened to us and answered our prayer
He is so faithful, He keeps His word

The two of us had a change of heart
We renewed our covenant…'till death do us part
The shackles were removed from our eyes
Again God was the center of our lives

CHAPTER 15
MY ALABASTER BOX

As I approached my eleventh year of marriage to Eddie, it became obvious that I was "humpbacked" in the spirit. I had been carrying the same baggage for nearly 12 years. The weight was almost unbearable. Somehow I had managed the weight by shifting it and rearranging it, but never had I conceived I'd ever dismantle it.

I began talking to the Lord about it. I told him I was tired and weary. My journey had been a long and tedious one with so little joy along the way. I wanted to feel the living waters flowing through me as I had when I first accepted Jesus as my Lord and Savior. I wanted to feel free and to dance before His presence with joy. I told the Lord that I was ready to release it to Him. I didn't quite know how to let this awesome burden go. It had been such an intricate part of my life.

I thought about Pastor Mike and Pastor Kathy and how they often minister to our church body regarding the joy and release that comes through a transparent lifestyle. (God had also used them, as well as Pastors Nate and Valerie Holcomb, to restore my faith in pastoral leadership once again.) I began to meditate more and more on becoming transparent. The victory in becoming an overcomer after all these years was a desire that began to grow in me. Although the constant reminder of my failure was still before me, its impact was losing power to my increasing desire for freedom.

I shared with Eddie my desire to be free. He told me that he was in agreement, for he, too, wanted me to be released. Finally, I decided I would open my alabaster box. I was familiar with the weighty contents of this box all too well. It consisted of pain, unforgiveness, anger, failure, impurity, low self-esteem, fear, grief, and shame. My alabaster box was full and heavy. I wanted to exchange it, to empty its contents. "I am ready to be healed" I told the Lord. "I want to be completely healed." Shortly after saying this sincere prayer, things began to change in my life. I still had my alabaster box, but I could sense it would soon be emptied of its contents. My mind was being renewed as I slowly began to latch on to God's promises for me.

"For I know the thoughts and plans that I have for you, says the Lord, thoughts and plans for welfare and peace and not for evil, to give you hope and a future." Jeremiah 29:11- Amplified Version. God's promises are sure and Amen.

One day as Jill Blue, my Elder, and I were returning home from visiting one of our members in the hospital I decided to tell her about my past. To share my hidden 12-year secret was a courageous step for me. Yet, more than that, I felt to do so was to begin the process of opening my alabaster box. As she was talking I was trying to determine the approach I would take in disclosing my story. At first, we talked about many topics in general. Then, without delay I told her I would like to share something. Jill responded "sure". I paused for a moment, I knew this was it, I had no plans to change my mind. I was going to tell her my secret no matter what. I had Jill's undivided attention as she sat there waiting for me to begin. And so I did. From the beginning to the end. As a matter of fact, before we knew it, we were parked in front of my house.

Jill's response was so gentle and so reassuring. Her words confirmed that my character over the years had been such that I could not be compared to the woman in the story of which she was hearing. "Pat, it's like you are telling me about someone else, not you, there is nothing about you that would ever make me think that," she softly spoke. Her words of affirmation comforted me as she remarked that I now walked in a manner diametrically opposed to where I had once been. Jill continued to listen, offer support and give comforting words as I became more emotional.

As I concluded our conversation, I told her that I was thinking about writing a book to help other women who might be familiar with the same type of shame and bondage, for I myself had no one I knew of who could relate personally to this difficult journey. There had been no one who could give me their success story on how they came out of such a degrading situation from within the church. During my darkest hours, I had so needed to hear how someone else made it through my own type of ordeal and agony. Yet, I had never heard a testimony, seen a book or even an article which addressed the issue of the shame and the battle of overcoming such an incident.

I gave Jill a quick hug. She thanked me for sharing my story and agreed that should I write a book, for it would bless women who needed answers and consolation. Jill also commended the husband that God had given me. "Yes, Eddie is my gift from God" I told her.

As I approached my front door, I felt such a sense of victory. I had done it! I had disclosed my darkest secret. At this point, my alabaster box lay open. I peered inside ... fear was no longer there.

Section Three
Finality/Conclusion
(Number Nine in Scripture)

CHAPTER 16
SATURATED WITH HIS WORD

In the midst of my determination to speak out about my past, contemporary gospel artist, Vickie Yo'e, came to our church. An anointed gifted woman of God, she ministered in song. God began to use her music to bring healing and strength to my spirit. I purchased the two tapes with the songs that ministered to me. I played these songs over and over again, "Hold Me Like A Baby" and "The Mercy Seat". As I would play "The Mercy Seat" while at home alone during the day, I would literally see myself running to the mercy seat of God and I would sometimes even act out my entry into His presence, kneeling at His mercy seat. For there, in His presence, I knew I would find my healing. I did this several times a week for three weeks continuously. As I did so, I actually began to feel healing and restoration take place in my life. The time spent with the Lord in praise and worship and listening to these songs became a time of transitioning into my complete healing. I could feel it. The process was slow and steady. God was doing a new thing in me and I knew it!

Vicki Yo'e's visit to Covenant Church laid the foundation for me to participate in BOW, "Band of Women" at Covenant Church. Pastor Kathy introduced this new ministry to our ladies. BOW came into existence as a result of a conversation Pastor Kathy had with her mother, Molly Parker. Ms. Molly was telling Pastor Kathy that women need to know how to pray. She stressed that women needed to be taught how to pray effectively so as to reach heaven, the very throne room of God. As Pastor Kathy listened to her mother, God birthed BOW in her spirit. BOW not only gave women the opportunity to strengthen and energize their prayer lives as they infiltrated and overcame the powers of darkness, but BOW also provided women the opportunity to attend classes centered on contemporary, relevant women's issues within the context of a thorough, comprehensive study of God's Word.

The Lord specifically instructed me to attend the ladies BOW. He even freed my work schedule so it was not as booked at that particular time. Consequently, I was able to keep my mornings free so I could attend the prayer time and the class sessions. Pastor Amy Hossler was the teacher for the class "A Woman's Heart – God's Dwelling Place," the session I had elected to take (she and her husband, Pastor John are Pastors of our Children's Church and the Headmasters of our church school, AHA). Beth Moore authored the class materials. I did not know it then, but God would use this class to supernaturally change my life.

Through Pastor Amy, God taught me to love His Word. As mentioned earlier, reading my Bible had been one of the biggest challenges in my Christian walk. I would open my Bible, perfunctorily read a scripture or even a chapter but while I was doing so, experienced extreme boredom, coupled with an accompanying sense of condemnation and frustration.

All my Christian life I had heard how I, as a Christian, needed to stay in God's Word, how powerful the Word was, etc. Though I tried, I never seemed to connect with God through His Word. Though reading the scriptures bored me, out of obedience, I faithfully read, hoping for illumination. Admittedly, my disinterested attitude further elicited a lackluster response to God's Word. Often, I would opt to read Christian literature and books, rather than ingest a steady dose of the Bible.

At the first class, Pastor Amy boldly prophesied over all her students that when we completed her class we would passionately love God's Word. She firmly believed this and spoke it over us. By the third class, I knew I was in the midst of a dynamic transition. I found myself reading more chapters from the Bible in just a few weeks than I thought possible. I studied and studied, yet never wearied. For one to two hours daily I devoured the Bible. With accompanying workbook in hand, I diligently recorded and studied reference verses as I researched and reveled in rhema truths previously foreign to me. Though each study session would take an hour to two hours to complete, I became oblivious to the time. Facts once considered dull, I now learned with vigor. My excitement intensified as I drew the ark of the covenant and memorized the location of the brazen alter, the brazen laver, the golden lamp stands, the Holy place and ultimately the Holy of Holies where the priest would meet God. I began to understand the Ark of the Covenant and most importantly, the mercy seat.

God had already been preparing me for the mercy seat through song and dance. Now, He arranged provision for my eventual freedom from my shackles of the past through the comprehension of His Word. As I studied, I would bask in His presence. And, oh, how I loved to be in His presence! As I wept before Him and learned His ways, <u>I was finally able to appreciate His love for me.</u> I did not want to reject anything about Him and wanted everything He had for me. As a result, I was finally able to relinquish my desire to be judge and jury of my life.

Jesus Christ assured me that I was worthy to be forgiven because **HE** counted me worthy. I'll never forget the moment that my soul laid bare before Him at my dining room table as I studied. My alabaster box was still full, yet some elements fragmented. An overpowering desire surged throughout my body and I yearned to give God everything. For I knew if I released the contents of the alabaster box, I would release the items that I had placed value on, the items that controlled my life. Everything that I had made more valuable than Him, I wanted to release and give to Him. Just as the woman who had an expensive vial of oil in her alabaster box used it to anoint the Lord, so I too, would use the contents of my box as a humble offering to Jesus. All my years of sorrow and shame were laid at the cross of Jesus. I could feel the love from my Savior flood my soul to the point that I felt a release to <u>finally forgive myself</u>. I actually wanted to forgive Patricia for her failures. It was really okay, I told myself. I could forgive my failures, I didn't have to walk in the condemnation of my past any longer. The pain, the anger, the failure, impurity, low self-esteem, grief, shame and unforgiveness all came under the blood as I sat at my dining room table and wept and wept. My study guide, my bible, and my music all accompanied me that day as I accepted my freedom through Christ Jesus. I left my alabaster box at the foot of the cross that morning as I lay before Him. The blood of Jesus had cleansed me and washed me from head to toe. No longer just a verse in the Bible, His Word truly was a lamp to my feet and a light to my path. I could actually see my way clearly. To be in His Word was to be in His presence.

All these years I had been missing out on loving God's Word. Now, I finally understood what people meant about the Word! I became saturated in it. I was absorbing His Word and His Word was absorbing me. That morning in September, I had miraculously been healed of my past. Continuously transformed in my inner man, I continued in Pastor Amy's class for approximately three months from beginning to end.

While in her class, Pastor Amy played a tape by Integrity Music called "Shout." The song that most ministered to me was "Jesus, Lover of My Soul". In total, I played that song at least 20 times a day, if not more. As I did so, its message permeated the very depths of my being and I knew, without a doubt, that God truly loved my inner man, my soul, the part of me that must constantly die daily. What a blessing to know God loved the soul of man.

THE RHEMA WORD

*All my life I had been taught
that by Jesus' blood my life was bought
To read and study my Holy Bible
for through God's Word would come revival*

*And so I practiced religiously
reading His Word so faithfully
I thought how God would be proud of me
for taking the time to stop and read*

*But though His Word was in my head
I did not absorb it has my daily bread
It was not hidden in my heart
To rightly divide His Word apart*

*And then one day in my search
I began to hunger and to thirst
For all His Word had for me
I turned each page so desperately*

*Soon living waters flowed out of me
And I knew my past would be my destiny
God's word came alive, stood strong and tall
And down came every barrier and every wall*

*I forgave myself for what I had done
And with new vision, a new life begun
In me and through me I knew I was free
Through the Rhema Word, I had the Victory!*

CHAPTER 17
THE AUDIBLE VOICE OF GOD

While still a student in Pastor Amy's class, the Lord laid on my heart to do a three day liquid fast. Inwardly, I felt God calling me to a new area of ministry, but I was unable to identify just what it was. My gifts and talents had previously been utilized in the area of my creative abilities. I now pondered whether God was calling me to write plays again. As the previous drama director with the Youth Ministry under the Pastoral leadership of Pastors Gordon and Derozette Banks, I would write skits (when I would permit myself), but it had become increasingly difficult to maintain my focus in that particular department because I knew God was redirecting me. I wanted to do what He wanted me to do, not what I thought I should do.

On the third day of my fast, a voice awakened me early in the morning. In a gentle, yet authoritative voice, I heard the words: "Patricia ... it's 3:00 o'clock!" I sat straight up in the bed when I heard it and looked at the clock, it was indeed, 3:00 a.m. I turned around to my husband to see if he too, had been awakened, but Eddie was sound asleep. There was no mistake, I was awakened by the audible voice of God. His voice was distinguishable—I knew I hadn't dreamt it. As I fell back on my pillow, I silently whispered, "Lord is that you?" I waited silently, it was still and quiet once again. What a peaceful feeling, that God had awakened me. But "why?" I thought as I tossed and turned before slowly drifting back to sleep.

When it was time to arise the next morning, I distinctly remembered the still, small voice. So, I turned to Eddie and asked him if he had called out my name at 3:00 a.m. (I knew he hadn't, but I just wanted to hear him say "no"). Eddie confirmed that he had not. I told him what had happened and that I knew it was God's voice speaking to me. However, I didn't have a clue as to what the words, "Patricia ... it's 3:00 o'clock" meant.

The next morning when I went to Ladies B.O.W., I wrote Pastor Amy a note and explained what happened and asked her if she knew what this message meant. I left the note with one of her assistants to give to her. After this, I decided to keep a journal of dates so that I could record anything the Lord might speak to me.

On the night of October 1st as I slept, I was awakened again. But this time it was Satan. He said to me twice... "Shame, Shame." It was the slimiest, most pitiful voice ever. Low in volume, it was spoken directly into my ear, as though he was just inches away. He sounded desperate, as he was fully aware that he had lost his grip in my life. Then he quickly vanished as I called out the name of Jesus. I continued to cast down the words that he spoke over me. I knew he was trying to put the weight of shame back on my shoulders again. I knew I would have to continue to fight Satan for my right to stay free.

The next morning I told Eddie what had happened. I told him that Satan was well aware that he had lost and that he was trying to reach out one last time. Speaking "shame" over me no longer had the power it used to. His words were very weak, almost lifeless. "Shame" was left at the foot of the cross that morning in September at my dining room table. I refused to pick it up again. However, I could sense the remnants of the tattered veil-it was trying to linger.

I HEARD HIS VOICE, GOD SPOKE TO ME

*As I slept, I heard God's audible voice,
I heard Him call out to me.
"Patricia", he said, "It's 3:00 o'clock"*

*Could it be that He would call my name?
<u>Who am I</u> that He would think of me?
And why me?*

*His voice was gentle, yet He spoke with such purpose.
He was calling me to do something
He was calling me....*

*I'm not for sure what 3:00 o'clock means
So I inquired and then discovered that 3:00 o'clock
was a time of purpose, destiny, appointment, if you will.
God was calling me to attention, He was specifically calling me*

*I humbly submitted myself to His Lordship,
"I am yours to use, thank you for counting me worthy in your sight"
He then told me my hour would come
to lay down my life and to pick up my cross*

*"I will" I said, for "<u>You</u> <u>alone</u> are <u>worthy</u>."
The appointed time came,
And I picked up my cross
to follow Him.*

*"...If any man will come after me, let him
deny himself, and take up his cross, and
follow me. For whosoever will save his life
shall lose it: and whosoever will lose
his life for my sake shall find it." Matthew 16:24, 25*

CHAPTER 18
THE POWERLESS VEIL OF SHAME

The following Tuesday after giving Pastor Amy the note, I saw her while I was volunteering at my children's school. She told me that she had received my written message of inquiry and wanted to share with me the symbolism of the 3:00 o'clock hour. She stated its prophetic implications. She told me that Jesus died at the hour of 3:00 o'clock (p.m.). Also, those who walk with a prophetic anointing arise at 3:00 o'clock to pray. She said that God often wakes her at exactly 3:00 a.m., so she can pray or read. She said it is an hour God chooses to get one's attention and stated that it was significant that God spoke this hour of time to me. She encouraged me to seek his face at 3:00 o'clock in the morning.

I wanted to both simultaneously run and weep. Oh, that God would speak to me ... oh how I loved Him so! God had spoken to me with a purposed message! He wanted me to do something, He wanted me, Patricia Harris, a fallen yet restored woman, to do something for Him! I had to share this joy with someone because I knew I could not contain it, it was so overwhelming! I then saw Jill, who is my elder as well as the School Director. I went into her office and jubilantly shared my good news with her. I told her how God had spoken to me at 3:00 o'clock in the morning. I then recounted to her what Pastor Amy had said. No, I didn't know what God was doing, but God was truly in control. Whatever it was, I was willing to do it. "Here I am Lord, send me"! was all that my spirit could say in humble surrender.

As our class came to an end, Pastor Amy spoke a prophetic word over the women, a word which I personally received and guarded closely. She prophesied that God was going use us as first fruits in the church and that God was going to bless us to do first things, things that had not yet been done. I held onto that Word. For 12 years, prior to this special time of transition and radical change, I had missed out on what God had wanted me to do. But now I was available, and whatever He wanted to do in me and through me, I wanted as well.

My revelatory conversation with Pastor Amy occurred the week of Covenant Church's Fall revival. I could sense the enemy trying to remind me in a subtle way of the all too familiar shame. I decided I would go up for prayer that night in an attempt to obtain pastoral covering as I continued to release lingering tattered remnants of the veil of shame. I told Eddie that I was going up to the altar for prayer and my reason, and he joined me in agreement. While at the alter I asked an usher to beckon Pastor Jessye (the Associate Pastor who had given Eddie and me counsel regarding demonic spirits approximately ten years ago) to come pray with me. He was able to get her attention and she came over.

(Though Pastor Jessye had been aware of my sexual impurity, she had not been informed until now that I had been involved in an affair with a pastor). In short detail I shared my past with Pastor Jessye. I explained that it had been 12 years since my affair with Pastor and I wanted the remnants of the shame to be completely broken off. Pastor Jessye prayed a powerful prayer. She began to violently "break off " in the spirit the hidden shame of my past and voiced a vigorous prayer of war in my behalf as well. She ministered to me and told me that she always knew God had something great planned for me but she never said anything because it wasn't time. She expressed that God had given me a spirit of counseling so that I could minister to others.

That night became a milestone leap in my spirit. This time the remnants and the entire veil of shame laid crumpled at the cross. There were no lingering tattered pieces remaining.

CHAPTER 19
UNASHAMED

The following month while attending a monthly leadership meeting, the topic being discussed at the close of our meeting centered on transparency with one another and with those whom we lead. Our Elders, Wayne and Jill, shared their own personal testimonies regarding their past. As they did so, the Holy Spirit suddenly prompted me to openly share in this intimate forum, my past. Before I said anything, I leaned over to Eddie and told him what I felt led to do. He nodded and took my hand.

I interjected that I had a story to share as well. As I began, I became emotional. (After 12 years of shame and always feeling that I would die with this deep dark secret hidden inside me, here I sat among leaders in a meeting to share the most intimate of details regarding my shameful past. I knew the timing was right, and I knew I was an unashamed woman. God had completely healed me and I wanted to share what he had done for me. I wanted them to know where I had been and where I was going). As the tears streamed down my cheeks, as they so often had in the past when I referred to this topic, I found myself crying for a different reason than before. This time I cried because I had experienced the healing of God and could now share my deep dark past as a testimony unto Him.

The tears not only streamed down my cheeks, but down the faces of some of those twelve leaders in the room as they listened intently to my story. I felt such genuine love and acceptance in that room as I told them of my initial refuge center, Christian House of Prayer, then later of Covenant Church and Pastors Mike and Kathy and their effective teaching on a transparent lifestyle. I referred to Pastor Amy's teaching, revealed how Pastor Jessye had broken off the chains of shame, how my oldest sister, Sherrie, stood in the gap, how my parents loved me unconditionally, and most importantly, how Eddie loved me and stood by me through it all.

After sharing my story, a hidden, shameful secret buried inside me for 12 long years, I felt judged by no one, just deeply loved. After I finished, Eddie encouraged me to tell them of my plans to write a book. So I shared with them that I felt impressed in my spirit that God wanted me to share my testimony as a witness to help other hurting women and perhaps, even men, caught in the web of sexual impurity in the church. I was well received that night and I knew I had embarked on a journey with God, He was indeed taking me somewhere that would require trusting Him and completely giving my all to Him, my Heavenly Father. This disclosure in this small setting was just the beginning of the many disclosures to come. Whether or not I would be well received as I had been at this meeting was questionable. However, to put things in perspective, it was not for me, it was for Him. There would be others who would need to hear my testimony so their captive souls could also be set free to proclaim an "unashamed" declaration.

(During subsequent leaders' meetings, my fellow leaders never treated me any differently. It was as if I had never told them. I thank God for His people – for their maturity, unconditional love and covenant relationship.)

That night after I returned home, I turned to Eddie and told him that I felt like I was on an indescribable high! It was, I continued, as if the larger the audience I shared my testimony with, the more grace. I experienced twelve years/4380 days of my life battling with the shame and the unworthiness, but now, as a part of my healing, I walked in the liberty of God's grace to unashamedly and openly share my testimony. Hopefully, one day soon, I confided to my husband, it would be told for the healing of countless others.

As confirmation of the desires of my heart, the Lord, in December, instructed me to pen my story the following January and that He would anoint me to complete it. In obedience, I blocked out the designated dates in my calendar to begin the writing of my book.

By proclaiming that one is "unashamed" it does not imply that one is in any way proud of their shameful past, but rather it is a declaration to the enemy that states: "I will not be marked as a failure, as one who must wear a veil of shame. I've been bought by the blood of the lamb and am counted worthy! I will not walk as though I have no hope. For I am victorious, I am unashamed in the eyes of my Father, He is proud of me!"

FROM SHAME TO GLORY

There are no adequate words to describe the journey
from a veil of shame to a veil of glory
I can only tell you that it has taken 12 long years
For me to finally be able to tell my story

My mind takes me back to just before my fall
At the point where I was caught in between
Caught up in a whirlwind of flesh
Living in fantasy and dreams

Thinking the grass was greener on the other side
Wishing I could taste of the forbidden fruit
Feeling vibrant and alive again
Willing to accept a lie instead of truth

When I think back on all my folly
And the future that was 12 years ahead
There is no way I could have ever known
The shameful path I would tread

The beauty that I can see in this
Is that God turns bad into good
Only he can bring forth some positive
Out of what no one else ever could

And for years I wore a veil of shame
Until the time of my release
When it was then quickly removed
And the havoc and torment was ceased

Upon my head God placed a new veil
It was gorgeous and white as snow
It was trimmed in gold, and sequenced pearls
With diamonds all in a row

And every where that I turned my head
The demons would cover their eyes
They would yell and cry out for mercy because
The veils' glory was their deathly demise

They knew that they had lost the battle
And it was over for their tormenting games
Because under my feet all crumpled up
Was the destroyed veil of shame

"Here! Take it now!" And I threw it down
where it rested it at their feet
"Now pick it up and put it on
And wear it as a sign of defeat!"

And at my command they put it on
This wretched 12 year old veil
"You'll wear that in shame from here on out
Now depart from me and go to Hell!"

And so my story ends with this
I am no longer ashamed
I've been washed in His redeeming blood
I am victorious in Jesus' name!

CHAPTER 20
HURTING WOMEN, HEALED LIVES

During the Christmas season, my husband, children, and I went home to share the holidays with my parents and siblings. While there, the Lord spoke to me and told me that my ministry to women would connect with the non-profit organization, **Women Who Love God's Way, Inc. (WWLGW)**, founded by my mother, Mary Cunningham. **WWLGW** is a non-profit organization founded to bring spiritual restoration and guidance to hurting women. The theme for this non-profit organization, "Hurting Women, Healed Lives", reflects my mother's own tender heart for hurting women.

Always a great mentor, who believes the best about everyone, I can still remember the sensitivity in my mother's response when I finally told her about my affair with Pastor. Amidst the shock, hurt and her obvious disappointment, she praised me for getting out of the relationship. Over the years, my mom never rejected me, nor brought it up as an issue of rebuke. She just continued to love me as she always had. A man of few words, my father simply listened, loved me and, like Mom, expressed his relief that I had gotten out of the situation. My parents are such jewels. I love them and I am glad they have always been there for me. It is because of their belief in me that they invested in the first printing of this book.

After sharing with my mother concerning the release I felt to write this book, she requested that I be one of the speakers at the WWLGW Annual Conference to be held in the fall of the upcoming year. She wanted me to give my testimony and minister healing in the lives of other hurting women, women who might be dealing with bitterness, shame, self-condemnation and/or other painful, often unspeakable issues from their past. Free from my own chains of shame and self-condemnation, I could now look forward with joyful anticipation to the opportunity to share and impart the beauty and reality of God's amazing grace. For I now knew in my spirit that those 12 lost years would be redeemed over and over and over again at the expense of Satan's kingdom. He will pay a hundred-fold for every day of shame I endured. The exchange will be the equivalent of souls for the days I lost as a captive to shame. Since I was imprisoned for 4380 days, Satan will grimace as he sees a minimum of 438,000 captives set free! These women (and men) will be snatched from the grip of Satan! We will crush his head under our feet and with a loud shout, we will all declare, "I am healed by the blood of Jesus, I am unashamed!" Each time I get the opportunity to give my victorious testimony to the Glory of God, more and more territory will be taken away from Satan! And the gates of hell will not prevail against God's purpose and plan! To God alone be majesty, dominion and power!

HURTING WOMEN, HEALED LIVES

*For hurting women, God has a plan
You're not forgotten, He understands
He knows exactly where you have been
He knows the nature of your sin*

*But remember this, He's full of grace
He wants to know you face to face
You have no reason to run and hide
It's for your sins, His Son has died*

*The devil will try to feed you shame
To make you feel all disdained
But to him turn a deafened ear
And push him far, don't let him near*

*Remind him of God's written word
That when you pray, your needs are heard
Let Satan know you are not worried
'Cause through God's Son your sins are buried*

CHAPTER 21
CONCLUSION

As time with you, dear reader, draws to a close, please allow me to reveal some of the hidden secrets that God has since manifested to me. For instance, the Lord told me that the writing of the book you currently hold in your hands was my "3:00 o'clock hour." In essence, this was my hour to die to self, so that HE might be glorified. To write this book was to bare my soul ... and for Him it has been worth every shed tear as I traveled back in time to recount my past. Every sin that I laid bare before you has already laid naked at the cross of Jesus, covered under His atoning blood. With my veil of shame gone, and my veil of glory in place, I can now declare overcoming victory through Jesus Christ. You too, have a 3:00 o'clock hour. Listen for His voice and harken to His call. He has not forsaken you.

I feel it's important to let you know that "unforgiveness" towards yourself or others, will give Satan legal access to your life. Even though I had been delivered from the incubus spirit, I still experienced subtle demonic attacks from Satan throughout my years of shame. It wasn't until I totally forgave myself and allowed God to completely restore me, that I had dominion over the powers of darkness. They no longer have legal access to my life. Without an access key, Satan cannot get in. Remember that unforgiveness and sexual sins are two of the keys that give Satan legal access to your life to bring torment. It is also important to note that Satan has different plans for different ones. He specifically targets the people of God that He fears will be used to destroy His evil works. If Satan is riding your back about your failures and/or constantly tormenting you, then know this, God has great plans for your future! All you have to do is put Satan in His place by putting Him out of your life.

Based upon my experience with the powers of darkness, I have no fear because I have learned that Satan's greatest enemy is one who is armed in the power of the Word. Satan knows I am armed and dangerous. I am lethal where He is concerned.

God explained to me why He chose our daughter's name, Amazing Grace. He told me that she was named as a reminder to me of His amazing grace in my life. In the Old Testament, names were given to children for a purpose or as a reminder. For instance, Pharaoh's daughter gave Moses his name because he was drawn out of the water. Hannah named her son Samuel, "Heard of God" because, she had asked the Lord for a son and God heard her plea. So it was with our daughter, her name was given as a reminder to me of His **_amazing grace_** in my life.

God's grace also covered me as I wrote this book. Satan tried to discourage me and even tried to attack my children to cause me to lose focus. But through God, our children walked out in victory and I kept on writing.

Our oldest daughter is 17. Her name is Denyel. She is such a gracious young lady and possesses such fine qualities. Ever since Denyel was a little girl, she has had a heart for God. Though raised with Christian values, Denyel has been challenged in so many ways. We believe the enemy's plans were to use my divorce from her father, Fred Weaver, as a device to hinder her spiritual growth. As a sensitive and loving child, Denyel always sought to maintain a relationship with her dad. However, over the years, Fred did not reciprocate and Denyel experienced great frustration and rejection over his lack of interest in her and his non-involvement. Though Satan tried to use this rejection against her, we believe that Denyel became stronger and more committed than ever to walk hand in hand with God. Denyel, too, has a story she can share with other teenage girls, one that will help them stay focused and walk in purity. We are proud of Denyel. She has encouraged me as I have engaged in the writing of this book. Her main emphasis has been for me to follow the voice of God. She told me once, "I'm not worried about people knowing about your past, I love you Mom, and you will always be my mother." She further stated, "After knowing more about your story, I have a better understanding for the reasons you have always been so protective of me." Our girl, Denyel, has revealed that God has told her that she will use her gift of dance and song to glorify Him. She is excited about this new path that God is taking her on and shows more commitment everyday to be all she can be for Him. God has great things in store for our daughter, Denyel.

Our teenage son, Earl, is 16. He is such a precious jewel to God and he too, has been supportive about me sharing my story. Although, he initially expressed concern over what others would say about me, he quickly received a revelation regarding how my story would free others from shame. As I shared with Earl the dynamic transformation I had experienced from shame to unashamed he became more aware of God's influence in the publication of this book. He was also very touched by the story I shared regarding Eddies' love for me and how he cared for me in spite of my past. I expressed to Earl, his father (Eddie) encouraged me in the writing of my story. Earl who had never heard the full story of his father's sacrificial love for me until recently was further convinced that God's purpose and plan regarding the writing of this book must be preeminent. He told me I had his support and his love. Earl is anointed as an oracle for God. He possesses leadership skills and the innate desire to fulfill his purpose and destiny. We expect the manifestation of the call God has on Earl's life to be used as an influence for his peers and other young people.

Amira (Amazing Grace) our youngest, almost 11, understands the importance of purity and knows in general about my story. She is aware the content of this book is relevant to helping others overcome in the area of shame. Amira is an intercessor and has received a prophetic word that she has the spirit of Esther. In fact, Amira has been interceding for the birth of this book.

As you know, God has given me a wonderful husband, Eddie, a man who has been my covering from the very beginning. I am blessed as a woman of God.

May God enlighten your path and give you sure direction as you step out of your prison walls to walk in the liberty of your freedom through Christ Jesus. He has great plans for you. Don't let Satan bluff you by thinking your sin is too great to reveal. When you shed light on something, it is no longer hidden, but rather, it is illuminated and becomes visible for all to see. Where there is light, darkness cannot dwell. Let the light of Christ shine on your hidden secret. Make it known to Him by confessing it, then release it to Him. And Satan, who lives in darkness, will flee because he cannot stand to be in the light.

You are forgiven by God. Now it is time for you to forgive yourself. How? By knowing Him face to face through an intimate relationship with Him. Spend time with God, and let His Word permeate your being, your inner man. Thus, you will be able to leave your shame at the cross and walk in victory. And others <u>will</u> overcome by your testimony.

For this is a prosperous year for us. The doors of success have been opened. We shall succeed in everything in Christ. The door of failure has been closed and we shall not know defeat. Being fully persuaded that what He has promised, He is able also to perform.

EPILOGUE

As I close, I wish to again thank Pastor Jerry Parsons with whom I consulted regarding the writing of this book. He advised that instead of writing a partial transcript for submission to a publisher, that I actually complete it. He felt the writing of the book would also add to the completion of my healing and he was right. Thank you, Pastor Jerry, for your wise counsel.

God gave me a confirming Word a few months before it was time to publish this book. It came through a prophetess named Nancy, who was not aware of my past, and who ministers all over the nation. Nancy, by the Spirit imparted God's prophetic Word to me. I am writing in part what God has released me to share with you. It is as follows:

"For the Lord said, 'Your heart has been healed' and the healing that you have received graciously and freely of Him, you're going to freely give away to others who still have wounds in their heart. He's going to put their hearts in your hand. And those who would not trust anyone else with this issue of their heart will trust you. The Spirit of the Lord says, 'because they'll see the healing that's in your heart and they'll desire and hunger and thirst after that for their own lives'."

After this Word was given to me (which had been taped), I wrote it down word for word as it was spoken. God reminded me again of his promise:

For I know the thoughts and plans that I have for you, says the Lord, thoughts and plans for welfare and peace and not for evil, to give you hope and a future. Jeremiah 29:11

Several months before this prophetic Word came to me, I was contacted by the office of Pastors Mitch and Melinda Manning, the Pastors for the Family Development Ministry at Covenant Church. I had previously provided

Pastor Melinda with a copy of the manuscript for this book so she could write a prayer as an inclusion. (Her written prayer, among those submitted by others, is included in the prayer section of this book). Her secretary, Darla, e-mailed me to see if I would share my story in the fall for the Lady's BOW ministry. I'll never forget the feeling that came over me as I read my e-mail on that day. I was never so humbled and so blessed. To be able to sow a spiritual seed back into the BOW ministry, the ministry God had foreordained to start the process for my "freedom". To minister for BOW was a high honor.

I humbly accepted the invitation. I knew I would title the class: "From a Veil of Shame to a Veil of Glory". I envisioned women being set free by the healing of God's Word. What a privilege that He would take my testimony and use it for His Glory. *(No wonder the enemy tried to deceive me with shame. He is such a liar).* God is going to set thousands of women free by this book. God reigns and Satan loses, once again.

God has been with me day by day over the past 12 years. He was with me in every valley and during every storm. The Holy Spirit was ever present to guide me, and the blood of Jesus was always available to free me. Where would I be if He didn't love me?

Thank you for taking the time to read my story and its victorious ending. Yet, in so many ways it is an unfinished book ... the greatest chapters are yet to be written. You too, will walk in victory. It is inevitable. God has inspired this book so that you will walk out of your shame, from Glory to Glory. God Bless You, my friend.

May the purpose and intent of this book accomplish what it was sent forth to do according to the plan and will of God, our Father. Amen.

PRAYERS OF AGREEMENT

God has directed me to request prayers of agreement that you can pray over yourself as you seek to walk out and stay out of sexual impurity. If you have ever experienced the shame of sexual impurity or the shame of failure, then agree with the prayer that is most applicable to your current situation. Know that God has a specific purpose for your life. Don't succumb to the voice of Satan when he tries to remind you of your past. You are commissioned by God to fight Him, destroy Him and take back what He has taken from you, and then expect a hundredfold return!

The following prayers are for individuals who may read this book and see themselves in its written pages. These prayers have been written by Pastors' wives, and one by my very own mother. Please apply them to your own life and be healed! The enemy will try to rob you of your peace, your victory, your healing and if you let Him, He will try to sway you from or even ruin your destiny. Don't allow Him the opportunity! Be set free and walk in your own veil of Glory as the Bride of Christ.

A PRAYER REFLECTING GOD'S FAITHFULNESS
(The Unbeliever's Prayer)
By Evangelist Mary Cunningham

Father God, I come before Your throne room of grace and in Your presence I lie at Your feet. Only You can wash me from all my ungodly deeds and from all impure thoughts. Father, I realize that You love me and You said though my sins be as scarlet, they shall be as white as snow; though they be red like crimson, they shall be as wool (Isaiah 1:18).

Lord I thank You for Your cleansing blood. I am submitted to You and I invite You to come in and give me a clean heart and renew a right spirit within me.

Father God, thank You for letting me know that if I call on Your name and believe in my heart I shall be saved (Romans 10:9). Thank You for telling me through Your Word that if I come to You, You will in no wise cast me out.

As I read Your Word and walk in obedience I know You will direct me and empower me to live a victorious life through You. I will no longer succumb to the desires of my flesh. My desires will be Your desires. I will turn to You for strength when I feel weak. Please give me the wisdom to defeat Satan when he tries to attack me. I will hide Your Word in my heart and will allow it to be a lamp to my feet and a light to my path. I am no longer defeated, I walk as one who knows my place in Jesus. I am the Righteousness of Christ. In You and through You I am victorious.

Thank You for delivering me out of a world of darkness. I will worship You all the days of my life. You alone are worthy Father, and it is for You that I live. I love You Lord.

Amen.

PRAYER OF REPENTANCE FOR THE SINGLE
(Spirit of a Virgin)
By Pastor Melinda Manning

Father, I come to You now in the name of Jesus repenting for the sin of unforgiveness in my life. Your Word tells me that if I confess my sin, You are faithful and just to forgive me and cleanse me of all unrighteousness. Jesus, I confess my unforgiveness toward myself and those who have hurt me. From this moment on I choose, as an act of my will, to forgive myself for hurting others, and violating my own body which is the temple of Your Holy Spirit. I also choose to forgive the other person(s) who participated with me in this sin.

Satan, I bind every evil spirit that would come to bring condemnation and try to keep me tied to my past. I loose the peace of God to flood my soul and erase those scars. May they only serve as a reminder of God's faithfulness to forgive.

I break every soul tie with those with whom I sinned and take back those parts of me which I gave away. I take these scattered pieces and present them to You for You to restore to wholeness. I will hold on to my restored purity until I am able to give myself to the mate that you have chosen for me.

Thank You, Father, for the cleansing blood of Jesus that washes me white as snow. I ask You now to give me the spirit of a virgin and I will live in purity all the days of my life.

In Jesus' Mighty Name,

Amen

A PRAYER FOR SELF-FORGIVENESS
(The Unashamed Woman)
By Pastor Amy Hossler

Father God, we thank You that You are the God of restoration, a God that loves us so much that You gave Your only Son so that we might be restored through forgiveness. Father, we know that a lack of forgiveness blocks the flow of Kingdom power. We know that Your Word says that we should forgive those who offend us since You forgave us. So we ask You, Holy Spirit, to enable us to choose to forgive.

Father God, Your Word says in Psalms 103:12 that as far as the east is from the west, so far have You removed my transgressions from me. Right now I take You at Your Word and I ask You to forgive me for all the wrong choices, and all the selfish desires that led me to choose to satisfy my flesh and need for approval. I ask that right now You would help me to forgive myself. Lord, help me to forgive myself for defiling Your temple, my body. Help me to forgive myself for enjoying the pleasures of the flesh. Help me to forgive myself for the deceptive pride of being desirable. I know Father God that You cleanse me for service to You and that You do not desire to leave me with the guilt of this past sin (Hebrews 9:14). 1 John 3:21 says, "If our heart does not condemn us, we have confidence toward God". Therefore, I forgive myself from my sin because you paid the price for me. Thank You Father for forgiving me through the blood of Jesus.

I also now choose to forgive _____. Lord, I realize that even though my resentment may be justified, it will only hurt me if I choose not to forgive him/her. I forgive _____ for taking advantage of my vulnerability and my weak will. I forgive _____ for not being strong enough to make right choices, even when I didn't make right choices. I refuse to hold a grudge towards

_____ and Jesus, I release them into Your hands right now. I ask Lord that You would lay the ax to the root of any bitterness or resentment that may be in my heart. (Matthew 3:10)

Because of Your great mercy Lord, I receive by grace Your forgiveness. And by Your great mercy and grace, I choose to forgive those who have hurt me. I declare Your Word in Isaiah 61:7 that instead of shame I will have double honor. Therefore, by Your grace I declare that I am an <u>unashamed</u> woman. I cry out as the Psalmist David did in Psalm 51:10-13

> *Create in me a clean heart, O God,*
> *And renew a steadfast spirit within me,*
> *Do not cast me away from Your presence,*
> *And do not take Your Holy Spirit from me.*
> *Restore to me the joy of Your salvation,*
> *And uphold me by Your generous Spirit.*
> *Then will I teach transgressors Your ways,*
> *And sinners will be converted to You.*

Thank you, Father God, that I am forgiven and You will use even my failures to ultimately lead others to Your merciful love. In Jesus' Mighty Name,

Amen.

PRAYER OF DISPLACEMENT FOR YOUTH/TEENS
(Fearfully and Wonderfully Made)
By Pastor Derozette Banks

Father, I confess that I have believed the lies and deceptions of Satan when he told me I had to engage in illicit sexual relationships in order to feel loved or to have value. Father I repent.

Father, I repent for rejecting Your perfect love and settling for the unsatisfying lust of Satan that he gave as a counterfeit, which brought me pain and rejection.

I confess that I am fearfully and wonderfully made and I am not rejectable, but I have been accepted in the Beloved, which is Jesus Christ. I choose to walk in the truth of Your love Father.

Father, I believe that every good and perfect gift comes from You, and You do not want to withhold anything good from me. The love I long for and have searched for illegitimately I now look to You to fulfill.

Father, You are greater than any void I feel in my heart. I ask You to come and fill that void now. I ask You, Holy Spirit, to come displace any dysfunctional personality trait such as being overly sophisticated, extremely shy, promiscuous, shameful, insecure, haughty, jealous, envious, controlling, rejected, angry, lustful, addicted, rebellious, and worthless.

I choose to no longer cloak myself in these traits.

Holy Spirit come wash over me, cleanse me, purify me, and clothe me in Your robe of righteousness. Renew my mind with peace and purity. Heal my emotions with Your security and strength. I choose to walk in Your healing and wholeness, no longer in brokeness. You, Father, alone satisfy me and I will follow after You.

Amen.

A PRAYER FOR DESTROYING SOUL-TIES
(Restoration and Covenant with God)
By Pastor Jessye Ruffin

Lord Jesus, I confess that I have morally sinned against You and participated in sexual uncleanness. I now understand that I am a living sacrifice created in Your image and for Your Glory. I recognize that I have been purchased by the Blood of Jesus and my life is no longer my own. I ask you to forgive me for my sin and cleanse me from all unrighteousness. Lord, I forgive <u>name of person (s)</u> for their participation in this sin. I now sever the soul tie formed between me and _____ and I also call back into my being all parts of my soul that are now resident within _____. Lord I send back to _____ everything we shared illicitly in our souls. I forgive all hurt and rejection, and I also release all disappointments suffered in the relationship. Father, I release_____ and speak Your blessing upon them. I receive Your forgiveness and restoration and make a covenant with You this day to live my life to Your glory. This day, I receive the spirit of virginity into my own soul and spirit, and make a commitment to forever cultivate purity in my life and in the lives of my descendents.

Amen.

To ensure confidentiality, some of the names used in this book were fictitious.

The author would like to thank you for sharing in the victory of her glorious transformation. Feel free to share her testimony with others and to recommend "Imprisoned" as a vital resource to those seeking to be free from the shame of their past.

The People the Lord has freed will return and enter Jerusalem with joy and gladness, and all sadness and sorrow will be gone far away. Isaiah 51:11 (New Century Version) NCV

Since we have been made right with God by our faith, we have peace with God. This happened through our Lord Jesus Christ, who has brought us into that blessing of God's grace that we now enjoy. And we are happy because of the hope we have of sharing God's glory. Romans 5:1-2 (NCV)

*Instead of your shame you will have a twofold recompense; instead of dishonor and reproach your people shall rejoice in their portion. Therefore in their land they shall possess double; ever lasting joy shall be theirs.
Isaiah 61:7 (The Amplified Bilble)*

"Only God can take our failures
and make them shine in the
face of the enemy."

Patricia C. Harris

Spiritan Press